MY HIGHLAND
KELLAS CATS

CW00828306

by the same author

CAT COUNTRY
THE BEAST OF EXMOOR

MY
HIGHLAND
KELLAS CATS

Di Francis

JONATHAN CAPE
LONDON

First published 1993

1 3 5 7 9 10 8 6 4 2

© Di Francis 1993

Di Francis has asserted her right under the Copyright, Designs and Patents Act,
1988 to be identified as the author of this work

First published in the United Kingdom in 1993 by
Jonathan Cape
Random House, 20 Vauxhall Bridge Road, London SW1V 2SA

Random House Australia (Pty) Limited
20 Alfred Street, Milsons Point, Sydney,
New South Wales, 2061, Australia

Random House New Zealand Limited
18 Poland Road, Glenfield,
Auckland 10, New Zealand

Random House South Africa (Pty) Limited
PO Box 337, Bergvlei, South Africa

Random House UK Limited Reg. No. 954009

A CIP catalogue record for this book is available from the British Library

ISBN 0–224–03608–4 (hardback)
ISBN 0–224–03961–X (paperback)

Phototypeset by Deltatype Ltd, Ellesmere Port
Printed in Great Britain by Mackays of Chatham PLC, Chatham, Kent

Contents

Illustrations

Dedicated to Lord John Doune, Dr Frank Turk, Colin Barclay, Professor Charles Thomas, Dr Andrew Kitchener, Merrily Harpur and Tomas Christie, without whose help and support the Kellas cats would not have been discovered and this story never told.

With special thanks to Graham Ferguson, Martin Archibald, Gary Middleton and George Watt without whom the story told in the second part of this book would never have taken place, and to my editor Tony Colwell for his help, encouragement and support throughout the writing of this book.

THE WAY IN THE WOOD

In the weird and ancient wood,
There are fairy lights that fall,
Never by the sunshine made,
And a flicker and a shade,
Where no substance is at all;
There are thrilling touches laid
By no hand on head and shoulder;
Things that peep from leaf and blade
And blossom, when there's no beholder;
And we walk as in a story
Through the gloom and through the glory
Of the weird and ancient wood.

Isa Craig Knox

Introduction

According to the natural history books, there are only two feline species living wild in the British Isles in modern times: the domestic feral cat, introduced by the Romans, surviving and breeding in frequently hostile environments in both town and country, unowned and uncared for, and the Scottish wildcat, *Felis silvestris grampia*, a magnificent and ferocious creature indigenous to Britain and remaining secretive and untamed, avoiding its traditional enemy – man. Even today the wildcat remains our least known native predator.

In 1983 I introduced in my book *Cat Country* evidence to suggest that another much larger feline existed in the wilder parts of Britain, a leopard-size, sheep-killing cat that was increasingly seen. Three months after the book was published a large catlike predator on Exmoor was hunted by a detachment of Royal Marine Commandos but the creature was never caught or killed.

It was not an isolated case, though it did attract the most public attention. In the years that followed a rash of similar sightings and police investigations were reported from the Highlands of Scotland to the moorlands of Cornwall. Some people suggested that the situation was the direct result of the 1976 Dangerous Wild Animals Act which attempted to halt the indiscriminate owning of exotic or wild animals. The Act laid down strict regulations aimed at poorly kept collections and at preventing individuals from keeping unusual pets, such as big cats, in insecure environments. Faced with strict licences, inspections and heavy fines, some owners released their exotic pets, leaving sometimes dangerous animals such as leopards to fend for themselves. No doubt some of the reported sightings have been of escaped, lost or cast out cats, but that alone could not account for all or even most of the incidents that I described in my book *The Beast of Exmoor* ten years after the most celebrated case.

Could Britain have its own native big cat species, a survivor from the Ice Age that has remained hidden, unknown to scientists until this century? I discussed the possibility in my book and backed up the theory with biological data.

Yet is it conceivable that a large indigenous predator could have escaped the notice of zoologists in such a crowded island environment? Anyone who would dismiss the idea as nonsense should know that, until very recently, indeed one has. Another mystery cat, smaller than the leopard-size sheep-killers but none the less ferocious, black and recognised by only a few gamekeepers who have shot them on estates in the Highlands of Scotland, was brought to the attention of the scientific world for the first time in the mid-1980s. When the first dead specimen was examined by the experts it was dismissed as a hybrid between a black feral domestic cat and a Scottish wildcat. Now they are not so sure. In no way could the new black wild cat be a sheep-killer; it is simply not large enough to tackle a full-grown sheep. But if one unknown feline predator can suddenly emerge, what chance that soon we will discover the true origin of its larger mystery cousins?

This book tells the story of that second mystery wild cat and how I became involved in its study, first by trying to get a sceptical scientific establishment to conduct some serious genetic research on the animal and then by daily observing my own live breeding pair, the first ever to be kept in captivity in Britain.

1

The New Mystery Cat

Gamekeeper Ronnie Douglas approached the snare, hoping to have ended the career of the predator that had been preying on the young birds in the Revack estate's pheasant rearing pens. For the past few days a number of the birds had been taken and it was his job to shoot or trap the culprit. If he was lucky, he expected to find the limp russet body of a fox, for foxes were regular villains on the Scottish Highland estate, although feral domestic cats, mink, stoats, and even badgers were also attracted to the semi-tame plump birds. Rarer unwelcome visitors were the pine marten and the Scottish wildcat, both species protected by law, but the most common raiders were classified as pests and therefore quickly dealt with once they had revealed their presence.

The gamekeeper had set traps around the pens the previous night and now he hoped he had caught the thief. If the snares were empty, then he would have to reset them until either the predator was despatched or else it moved on. The lethal wire noose had done its work, but the unfortunate occupant of the snare was not a fox. A huge black cat, the size of a fox, lay twisted in the undergrowth, its eyes milky blue with the sheen of death. Ronnie Douglas touched the animal cautiously with his foot to be sure it was dead before crouching down to release it. He did not fancy being within

3

range of the teeth and claws if the creature was still alive. He removed the wire and lay the body out on the grass to examine it.

The creature was twice the size of a domestic cat, a powerful looking beast with a gleaming black coat and thick muscular tail, but it was not only the size of the animal that impressed the gamekeeper. Even dead, it had a ferocious snarl, its black lips curled back, revealing huge fang-like canine teeth. Despite being familiar with the wild animals living in the countryside, Ronnie had never seen a beast like the big black cat that lay stretched out before him. He was relieved the animal was dead, and would not have fancied confronting such a creature in life. It was certainly a predator that he did not want prowling around the estate. Usually the unfortunate victims of his snares would be quickly disposed of, but Ronnie was curious about the identity of this formidable black cat. He put the body in a sack and slung it into the back of the landrover to take it back to his cottage. Someone was bound to know what the beast was and where it had come from. Then he continued with his normal morning duties; identifying that cat would have to wait. The hard-working gamekeeper just hoped that there weren't any other such beasts prowling the surrounding Highland forests.

Following media coverage of my research into mystery big cats roaming Britain, many landowners had contacted me, either to tell me they had seen big cats on their land, or else enquiring when they had all the necessary ingredients – woods, water and a plentiful supply of rabbits, deer and sheep – why they hadn't? I usually suggested to these letter writers that they should talk to neighbours and check through old newspaper files, and if they were persistent enough, people would eventually come forward and tell of their sightings. One such letter came from Lord Doune, the eighteen-year-old son of the Earl of Moray. John was a very enthusiastic cat hunter and our correspondence flashed across the border for a year before he wrote to inform me that his uncle had spotted a brown big cat bounding across the hillside behind his house. But the sighting was of less interest than a newspaper cutting that John sent me a few months later. It was from the *Forres Gazette* and dated 3rd June 1986, although he hadn't got hold of it until August. The headline asked 'Is Feral Cat The Beast?', and the article reported a number of people claiming to have seen a large black puma-like cat in the north-east of Scotland. Tucked into the centre of the article were the following words:

> Recently Grantown estate worker Mr Ronnie Douglas caught an unusual cat-like animal near Revack farm. That animal was much larger than a domestic cat and described by Mr Orbell [then Director of the Highland Wildlife Park at Kincraig] as tall with tremendously powerful hind legs. It was jet black and had large canine teeth.
>
> The Institute of Terrestrial Ecology were contacted about the find and Mr Orbell says it is possible that the animal and that seen in the Forres area may be linked.

The newspaper went on to suggest that the animal may be a hybrid or have escaped from somewhere.

The story of my Highland Kellas cats was about to begin.

As it was nearly three months since the article had been written, what had happened to the cat's body? What did it look like and how big was it? The paper described it as large: how large? It wasn't the size of a full grown puma but could it have been a cub? Had the carcase been destroyed, or was there still a chance of getting hold of the bones, especially the skull?

I contacted the editor of the *Forres Gazette* who told me that a vet by the name of George Rafferty had examined and photographed the carcase of Ronnie Douglas's big cat. The existence of photographs was exciting news. Even if the body had been destroyed, it still might be possible to identify the species. I telephoned Ronnie Douglas immediately. He said he had found the cat dead in a snare one morning, and besides being a monster of a cat with huge teeth, it had very long legs and coarse whiskers.

'How long was the animal?' I asked.

'Forty-three inches.' He had stretched out the carcase and measured it. Forty-three inches long and fifteen inches at the shoulder – a very rangy animal with a thick black coat and muscular bushy tail.

'Could it have been a young animal?' I asked.

Ronnie Douglas paused. 'Do you mean a kit?' he asked.

'Yes. The young of a much larger cat?'

'Not that young, no. It was a juvenile, I'd say, by its condition. About a year, maybe eighteen months, but it was a fully developed tom-cat.'

My heart sank. If it was a year plus and only forty-three inches long, then it certainly wasn't connected to the British puma-like cat which measured about five-and-a-half to six feet in length. And yet if it wasn't the cub of a big cat and didn't appear to be an ordinary domestic feral, then what was it? I asked about the photographs and he promised to send me copies. I also questioned the possibility of digging up the body to obtain the skull.

'Oh, you don't need to do that,' the gamekeeper said cheerfully. 'Dig it up or anything. It's with our taxidermist Ronnie Buchan. We had a few deer heads to send him, so we added the cat as a curiosity.'

Where else but on a Highland estate would people have their own taxidermist?

The photographs arrived a few days later – three reasonably clear pictures of an obviously dead cat. One showed the head raised up with a man's hand, just visible, clutching the poor beast by the scruff of the neck; another the carcase stretched out on the ground. The third photograph was a close-up of the open mouth, an attempt to record the large teeth. These were said to be Eddie Orbell's pictures: the vet's measured photograph (see p. 86–7) was shown to me for the first time years later when I had almost finished writing this book and Mr Rafferty had become a celebrity as the television vet.

The Revack felid was larger than a domestic cat and looked strikingly powerful. It certainly had very long legs and a slim elegant body, although the head seemed rather small in comparison with the overall size, but that could have been due to the unnatural position of the body. The animal's coat was dark and the fur seemed to be slightly flecked and coarse. It appeared to be an adult, probably a young adult, certainly not a cub. Though bigger than a domestic cat, it was too small to have any connection with the mystery leopard-size cats I was investigating. Could it be an escaped exotic?

Even if it was, the Revack cat didn't resemble anything I could bring to mind. The most common coat colours for the smaller cats are spotted, golden brown or tabby stripes. Black, known as melanism, does occur among the smaller species but it isn't common. All the same, looking at the photographs of the Revack Highland cat, I was struck by a similarity to other reports of strange cats sighted in the British countryside. Many of these I had dismissed as being just large domestic moggies. It is difficult for the average person to judge size in relation to distance, but some of the descriptions were very precise, the witnesses convinced that the creatures were not ordinary domestic cats. Some people living in northern Scotland could have seen true Scottish wildcats, although *Felis silvestris* has a fawn-to-grey tabby patterned coat and has never been recorded as black. One such sighting was by a Mr Weaver near Ashdown Forest in Sussex.

> I was walking along a grassy woodland path with a friend when we both became aware that about twenty yards in front of us, walking in the same direction, was a large black cat. We could hardly believe what we saw as it was about 18 inches high and very definitely alien to anything one would expect to see of the feline species in this country. The features about the animal that made a great impact on us were the shiny sleekness of the animal and it appeared to have a black bushy tail. We stopped our forward progress because it was so unexpected and a little 'scary'. Within seconds it veered off the path and disappeared down a bank covered with heavy undergrowth.

After the publication of my book, *Cat Country*, I had been contacted by the cartoonist and journalist Merrily Harpur who, fascinated by the subject because a friend of hers had seen one of the mystery big cats, offered to help me with the research. Merrily wondered whether there could be more than one species of unknown cat roaming Britain and now I appeared to have proof that there was. I rang the hotel in the Hebrides where Merrily was staying on holiday to tell her about the Revack cat and to ask if she would visit Mr Buchan the taxidermist, on her way back to London.

The situation was urgent for I did not know how far the taxidermist had proceeded. Modern methods of taxidermy use only the skull and the skin, the rest of the animal being constructed on a frame of wire with fibreglass moulded shapes. If work on the Revack cat had started, then the soft parts of the body would almost certainly have been discarded, but if the body was still in the freezer, we could perhaps obtain the whole animal for scientific examination. My hope was that Buchan had been too busy to start work on the carcase. So far my urgent letters to his address had gone unanswered and I had no telephone number for him.

Three days later Merrily arrived back in London and phoned me. The news was not good. She had eventually found the isolated cottage which she said was deserted. A large wooden door of an outbuilding stood open, and she had gone inside what appeared to be a workshop filled with stuffed and partly stuffed creatures. There was nothing resembling a large black cat. She had opened up some chest freezers, obviously used for storing carcases, and swiftly rummaged through them.

'It was horrible,' she muttered over the phone. 'All fur and feathers and blood, all in plastic bags! It was almost impossible to recognise what they were.'

She found no sign of the Revack cat, so where was it? Had the taxidermist ignored my frantic letters because he no longer had the cat and didn't like to admit it? I called Ronnie Douglas again and asked if the cat had been returned.

'We seem to have lost touch with him ourselves,' Ronnie told me. 'He was mounting a few other specimens for us

The New Mystery Cat

and they're all overdue. I'll let you know if the cat turns up.'

I thanked him and put down the phone. Then I sat staring at the photographs. Was this all that was left, the only record? What could have happened to the missing mystery cat?

While I was trying to trace the Revack specimen, the *Forres Gazette* was continuing to cover the story. Under a banner headline – 'Unknown Cat Shot In Morayshire!' – the entire front page was given over to reports of cat sightings, pictures of the Revack cat and quotes from various people, including myself. The editor, David Morgan, phoned to tell me that another cat the size of the Revack specimen had been discovered. It had been shot eighteen months earlier by Tomas Christie on the Kellas Estate. He had sent the carcase to a local taxidermist and this time the specimen had not gone missing. David Morgan had been to see it.

'It's a weird looking thing, I wouldn't fancy meeting it on a dark night,' he said. 'It's got huge teeth, though the animal is smaller than I expected. It also has a rather strange coat colour, black but with long white hairs flecked throughout. I don't know a lot about cats, but it's like nothing I've ever seen before.'

'Was it an adult animal or could it be a cub of a bigger cat?' I asked.

'Oh, definitely an adult,' he said confidently. 'It even had a tatty ear, as if it had been fighting.'

I was eager to go to Scotland to examine the Kellas specimen, but first I contacted Tomas Christie who had shot the animal. He assured me it was neither a wildcat nor a domestic feral cat and he'd killed at least four of them over the past couple of years. 'I thought this one was a rather fine specimen of whatever sort of cat it was I'd been killing,' he said over the phone, 'and worth preserving.'

'How did you come by it?' I asked.

He told me he had spotted it while out shooting foxes. 'There were two cats, presumably a pair, walking along by the river bank. I shot the one nearest to me, but its mate got away.'

9

'Were they the same?' I asked.

'I think so. The light wasn't good, but as far as I could tell the other one was dark. I think I've seen it since. It looks a little larger than the one I shot. Though of course I'm only guessing that it is the one that got away.'

'How many of them do you think there are?'

'Quite a few. As I say, I've killed several. To be honest, I didn't pay that much attention to them until I read about you and the Revack cat in the newspaper.'

'When you examined the carcases, what sort of ages would you say they were?'

Tomas thought for a moment before replying. 'Of the four I can immediately call to mind, one was definitely an adult and I'd say larger than the one I've got here. Another was very young, the size of a wildcat kit. The others, well, I'm not really sure about them. I just thought of them as rather odd fierce cats, a curiosity. My immediate reaction was to get rid of them as they were a threat to the birds. We kill foxes and feral cats for the same reason and my only interest in the black cats at the time was to dispose of them.'

He said I could go and look at his Kellas specimen whenever I wished. The next day I recieved some photographs from David Morgan and was able to look at the Kellas cat for the first time.

It had been mounted on a large branch in a snarling pose, one paw raised to strike, claws outstretched, ears laid back, the typical wildcat pose so loved by taxidermists, the thick bushy tail swept round the back legs. How it had looked in life I didn't know, but mounted it appeared terrifying. The most impressive feature were the teeth. The Revack cat had revealed very large fangs that jutted out below the lower lip, but it had been relaxed in death. The Kellas cat had its lip drawn back revealing enormous dog-size canines. I grabbed my own domestic cat and, despite its wriggling protest, examined its teeth. If the photograph told the truth, my domestic cat had tiny needles compared to the Kellas cat, and my pet was a fairly large neutered male. The Kellas cat's fur looked thick, black, and in very good condition. Scattered throughout the pelage, even the tail, were long coarse white guard hairs. I put the photographs of the Kellas and Revack cats side by side and studied them. They appeared to be similar. The Revack cat was wet, its coat muddy, with wisps of straw or hay visible where presumably it had been carried in a bag or sack, but closer examination under a magnifying glass revealed coarse long light-coloured guard hairs. Due to the colour distortion of the photograph, it was impossible to say if they were white or cream. Certainly the two cats looked very alike.

I really had to get to Scotland.

The national press picked up the story and I received a phone call from Breakfast TV. Would I be willing to do an interview about the animal? It was a difficult decision: I hadn't yet seen it and so I didn't feel I could say a lot about it, but if I didn't agree to appear on the programme no doubt someone with even less knowledge would be asked. I didn't watch Breakfast TV and had no idea of the format of the programme, nor even who the presenters were. But there was no time to worry about it; I said yes, and by four o'clock was on my way to London with the name of the hotel into which they had booked me for the night. I was to be collected by the studio car at six-thirty the following morning.

Before leaving I had phoned Merrily and arranged to see her that evening. Later, I was extremely glad that I did.

From the outside, the hotel looked pleasant enough though rather small, a typical Georgian terraced town house. I registered, collected messages and headed for the lift and my room. I couldn't find the lift, the only set of doors I could see led to stairs. I gritted my teeth, took a firm grip on my suitcase and started upwards. I later discovered that the lift was so small I had mistaken it for a broom cupboard. It accommodated two people with difficulty, three if they were very friendly.

Up and up I went until I reached the top floor, which in days past had been the attic. With a gasp of relief I slammed down my now heavy case, inserted the key in the lock, opened the door and entered.

The room was a small corridor measuring about four feet by ten with a window at one end. Directly opposite the door was a cupboard containing shower, washbasin and toilet. It was compact, to say the least but to use the washbasin you had to sit on the loo, to use the loo you had to sit with your feet in the shower, to use the shower you reached out to the washbasin for the extending water nozzle. The narrow bed took up one wall, the bedhead against the shower back, the telephone fixed on the wall above the pillows. There was a television set on a fixed shelf over the foot of the bed and a chair wedged between the end of the bed and the window. The only means of access to it was to climb across the bed for a fitted wardrobe jutted out from the opposite wall to touch the side of the bed. But it wasn't the cramped space that had an immediate effect on anyone entering the room. Everything – walls, ceiling, woodwork and floor – were all a bright terracotta red. It was like walking into a flaming passageway or a furnace. Or even hell!

I was speechless. Though not for long, I rang Merrily.

'I've arrived,' I said. 'You wait until you see the room.'

I had a shower to freshen up and discovered too late the lack of curtains, water cascading over the floor to lap against the toilet base. I threw down towels to mop up the lake and tried to turn off the water. I turned and turned, then wrenched frantically in the opposite direction, but still there was no response. Finally, by brute force, I got the flow down to a trickle but I couldn't get the water to turn off completely. I got dressed to the gentle trickling sound and went down to meet Merrily.

'Er, could you have someone see to my shower?' I asked the receptionist.

'Oh dear, won't it work?'

I nodded. 'Oh, it works all right. Trouble is trying to stop it working.' I also informed her that someone had forgotten to replace the shower curtains.

'They havent forgotten,' she said brightly. 'You don't have curtains in that room. I'll send you up some extra towels to lay on the floor.'

Merrily had arrived and I dragged her up in the broom cupboard lift to see my room.

'You've just got to see this,' I said. 'It's the most incredible place.'

'Good God!' she exclaimed as her eyes became accustomed to the glare. 'It's amazing.'

That, I felt, was an understatement. The small fridge was at least well stocked with alcohol and I could only suppose that anyone forced to spend the night in the decor had to be totally smashed to get through it and stay sane. Fortunately I was spending the evening with Merrily so I didn't need to revert to the fridge. On my return to the hotel at about two in the morning, I had an enlightening conversation with the night porter as I collected my key.

'My room is incredible,' I moaned. 'It's just a corridor. You couldn't swing a mouse in it, never mind a cat.'

He nodded. 'Top floor, are you?' he asked sympathetically. 'You must have one of the cabins. They are a bit cramped.' He passed me the key, noticing my number. 'Oh no, you're not in one of the cabins. You've got a *room*,' he said brightly. 'The cabins are smaller.'

I shall always regret my failure to knock up one of my neighbours and ask if I could look at a cabin. I can only assume they used hammocks.

Having asked for a five-thirty call, so as to be ready in time for the six-thirty car, I crawled into bed, swiftly putting out the light to hide the firy furnace, and slept. At five thirty the bell rang shrilly. I sat up with a start, remembering too late where the telephone was, directly over the pillows. The crack as my head made contact was loud enough to waken the neighbouring guests, even if the ringing hadn't. I jerked forward in the dark and a second crack sounded as I crashed into the TV shelf. I fumbled for the light and acknowledged the call. Still groggy from the combined effect of interrupted

sleep and being thumped twice on the head, I fell out of bed,
banging my knee against the wardrobe. I wriggled into the
shower, relieved to find it working, and liberally shampooed
my hair. Just as I had worked up a good lather, the water
suddenly began to get hotter and hotter. With a squeal I leapt
away from the scalding torrent, not an easy task with the lack
of space. Hastily I tried to adjust the temperature control but
it was hopeless. Whichever way I turned the knob, it made no
difference to the heat; the water was boiling and I was due at
the studio in half an hour. I poured toothmugs of cooled
water over my head but with little effect and toweled my hair
dry. There was no mirror anywhere in the bedroom area and
no electric point other than for a shaver in the bath-cupboard
where the only mirror was over the basin. There was nowhere
to plug in my drier and see what I was doing. I was standing
there, still damp and soapy, when the phone rang again. The
studio car had arrived early.

Perhaps studio make-up could do a quick salvage job.
Make-up was rather overloaded with work and so I did my
own. My hair still hung in damp greasy rats' tails as I was
shown across the littered studio floor and deposited on the
famous couch. It was just after seven. I glanced at the monitor
and decided not to repeat the action. I looked dreadful.

Frank Bough appeared from nowhere and sat next to me.
'Have you met our guest of the day?' he asked. I became
aware of the woman seated on the other side of me. 'Have you
met Joanna?'

What hope had I? Bruised, battered, starved, soggy, soapy
and seated between Selina Scott and Joanna Lumley! Two of
the most beautiful women in the country. Sometimes I think
life is against me.

I have been interviewed by a number of presenters over the
years but I have to give Frank Bough his due for he really does
provide an aura of gentle calm and genuine interest, rather
like a soft-spoken family doctor. Instead of being interviewed
in a conveyor belt situation, it was like having a quiet
informal chat with a favourite uncle.

Of course the new cat was confused with the large panther-like cat I was also investigating and a photograph of the Kellas cat was flashed up on screen together with references to the Exmoor Beast. I tried to explain in the very limited time I had that the two sorts of cat were not to be connected, though the Kellas cat didn't appear to be connected with any other known cat either.

I was asked if I would like to 'put it in one of Joanna's zoos?' Having not seen the start of the programme I had no idea that Joanna Lumley was there purely to publicise her fight against keeping animals in zoos. For the first time that day the gods smiled favourably on me. 'Oh, no! I want to put a tracking collar on one and return it to the wild,' I said.

By the afternoon I was back home in Devon, nursing a headache and worrying about getting up to Scotland to see the Kellas cat for myself. Then I received a call from Professor Charles Thomas in Cornwall. It was less a phone conversation and more like a direct collision with a velvet-lined steamroller. Charles Thomas is one of those brilliant academics who combines a successful career with an active interest in a hundred other happenings around him who assumes that everyone else has the same power source as he has, driving those around to greater efforts. He had read my book *Cat Country* with interest because, as a young boy at school near Okehampton, he had seen one of the big cats, and now, having noted the publicity about the Kellas cat, he wanted to know why I was still sitting on my butt in Torquay when I should have been heading north in a cloud of dust.

I explained tactfully that I was indeed going to Scotland but needed to get one or two things organised first. Charles was not a man to be fooled, nor was he a man to waste time on useless chat.

'Would the financial consideration be contributing to the delay?' he asked bluntly.

I hedged slightly. 'Well, there's that too.'

He said something about having a good year himself and then went on to ask me about the Kellas cat. The following day a cheque arrived in the post with a note simply signed 'A friend.' It was for a hundred pounds.

I phoned Merrily and told her I was on my way. She offered to come with me, a very acceptable offer since, due to her passion for murdering salmon, she knew her way around Scotland and where to find the Perthshire taxidermist. I still hadn't heard anything from him regarding the Revack cat.

Next morning, accompanied by a London-based cat enthusiast called Terry, yawning and bleary-eyed we faced the London dawn, and with the grey light filtering through the strangely empty streets we set out to drive north. For the first time in days I could relax. In a matter of hours I would actually see the Kellas specimen. We decided to make a stop at Kirk Michael in another attempt to trace the Revack cat's taxidermist, hoping that he would be able to examine both cats and compare them.

It was dark before we reached the taxidermist's remote cottage which was surrounded by dark creaking conifers. We staggered out of the car, stiff from our long journey, and surveyed the desolate scene. No cheery light shone from any window and the whole place looked abandoned. Gone were visions of welcoming cups of tea, but also gone were the fears of shotgun rejection.

'Come on,' said Merrily gamely. 'I've got a torch, so let's have a look round.'

She led the way, Terry and I stumbling over the rough ground in the wake of her torch beam. There was little doubt that the elusive taxidermist was likely to remain elusive a little longer, for the path was cluttered with black plastic dustbin bags and rubbish was heaped outside the front door. We shone the torch beam through the windows into empty rooms with bare floorboards. Our quarry was long gone. Just how long could be judged by the contents strewn out of some of the torn bags from which rose an appalling stench. One did not need the torchlight to recognize the evidence of the former owner's profession. Bags of rotting carcases littered the garden.

'There's his workshop,' said Merrily, bravely ignoring what squelched and crunched underfoot. 'That's where I went last time.'

Beside the house was a large stone building, its wooden door hanging open. Cautiously we tiptoed inside, feeling like criminals even though discovery of our crime seemed unlikly in the circumstances, and we certainly weren't breaking and entering, only entering.

Both floors of the huge barn were empty but for a few skins and half-completed mounted deer heads staring back at us unwinkingly from fixed glass eyes. It was spooky, the vault-like stone building echoing to the hollow thuds of our footsteps, the light playing with the shadows, suddenly catching the glint of watching eyes. We were relieved to get out into the chill night air away from the feeling of lurking menace. Having drawn a blank with the building, now we were faced with the horrors of the plastic bags. We played the light around the garden. A ghostly glimmer of white revealed itself to be an abandoned deep freeze unit, a huge rusting metal sarcophagus standing in isolated splendour in the centre of the garden. There was nothing for it but a quick poke into the decaying furry heaps in search of anything that even faintly resembled the mortal remains of a black cat. It was like a scene from a horror film, the three of us crouched in the isolated clearing between the black fir trees, lit by the cold light of the moon and the wavering yellow beam of the torch, digging and prodding through the death heaps of rotting flesh and disintegrating fur and feathers. The stink was appalling as bag after bag was shaken to disgorge the contents on to the ground while we dug around in the search for any black fur. There were some easily recognizable foxes, stoats, hares and squirrels, and other horrors that would have defied identification by anyone but a forensic scientist. However, there did not appear to be anything of the right size with black fur.

Finally, defeated, we gave up and turned to the huge chest freezer that stood in the middle of the garden. I looked at it uncomfortably.

'Do you think . . .?' I began.

'No,' said Merrily firmly. 'He would have emptied it before moving it. There won't be anything in it.'

I agreed with her, but suppose . . . I couldn't leave without being sure. 'Hold the beam on it and I'll just check.'

Merrily played the wavering light on to the ghostly white chest as I approached and, steeling myself, I grabbed the rusting handle to heave it up. As anyone opening a chest freezer will know, the act cannot be accomplished with a stand-back movement; one has to lean across the chest to push up the lid.

I was suddenly aware that it was raining. Heavy drops pattered down on my head and face, splashing on to my shoulders. Then I was hit by the most appalling stench, the ammonia hitting my eyes and throat at the same time, blinding and choking me. Tears streamed down my face as I fought for breath. The raindrops fell heavily. Then the air cleared and I was able to breath again. I opened my eyes and peered down through the mist of tears just as I heard Merrily give a horrified gasp. The whole interior of the chest heaved and rippled under a blanket of maggots, the contents buried in the pinky grey wriggling mass. But worse was to come. As I leapt back I realised it wasn't raining. The inside of the lid was also covered with a coating of maggots and in lifting it I had dislodged hundreds to fall on top of me. They landed in my hair, on my clothes, down my neck.

Having attempted to shake off my unwanted companions, I had a very quick half-hearted poke with a long stick at the seething mass in the fly nursery and then quickly gave up. If the Revack cat was in there, it certainly wasn't going to be discovered until the maggots had done their work, leaving behind cleaned and recognizable bones for species identification.

With the sickening scent of decay soaked into our hair and clothes, we trudged back to the car and the prospect of continuing our journey to Inverness. All I wanted was to wash and change my clothes. I kept itching and wriggling as I

slumped wearily in the passenger seat, certain that little
maggots were still circulating down my jumper.

We stayed overnight in Inverness and arrived next morning
in Forres and met the editor of the *Forres Gazette*. David
Morgan was a small dapper man in his thirties who wasted no
time and soon we were off, heading inland towards Kellas.
Within minutes of leaving the town we were deep into the
wooded countryside, the forested slopes of the hills folding
up into the distant high mountains like giant earth mothers
with their tiny children clinging to their heather-coloured
skirts. David Morgan chatted as he drove, telling us about the
sightings of panther-size black cats around the town.

'I suppose Tomas Christie's cat might be responsible for
the rash of sightings but it's nowhere near the size of animals
witnesses have been claiming to have seen,' he said.

Tomas Christie was waiting for us, a tall pleasant man who
greeted us outside the huge old house before leading the way
into an old stone outbuilding where finally I came face to face
with the mystery cat of Kellas.

My first reaction was one of disappointment. Although
larger than a domestic cat, the animal was a good deal smaller
than I had expected. It was mounted on a large chunk of
wood, semi-crouched in an aggressive position, one paw
raised to strike, claws extended, ears flattened, its mouth
open in a perpetual snarl, large white teeth in formidable
display. Small it might be but dangerous it certainly looked.
With most small cat species, one fears the claws but seldom
considers the bite; the bite of the Kellas cat was my first
consideration. The teeth were large and gave the impression
of being made of white china, more like those of a dog than
the weaker translucent teeth of a domestic cat. The animal
was long-legged and light bodied, a thin rangy cat with a thick
black coat and short clubbed bushy tail like that of a wildcat.
The hind quarters were broad and powerful and reminded me
of a hare. The head was small compared with the body and,
despite the massive fangs and ferocious expression, the short
muzzle appeared slightly snubbed. Although the coat was a

chocolate-hued black, across the whole pelage were scattered very long coarse white guard hairs, giving the fur a strange texture. There was a small white spot on the animal's chest and a greyish white patch on its underbelly. The whiskers were long, tinged brown and very stiff, like plastic bristles.

It was definitely not related to the big cat I was researching but it was equally as interesting in its own right for I had never seen anything like it before.

Tomas Christie said that gamekeepers on the estate had been trapping or shooting such cats as far back as anyone could remember. He had only sent this black cat to the taxidermist because he had thought the animal was a very beautiful specimen of the large strange black cats that had fascinated him ever since he had killed the first one years before.

Although the true wildcat (*Felis silvestris*) is protected by law, it can be trapped on estates where keepers trap foxes and domestic feral cats in the course of their duties to protect the game birds and snares cannot be made to discriminate between domestic cats and wildcats. It may seem a brutal system to a city dweller but, as most of the natural predators are now extinct in the British Isles, there is no natural way of controlling the numbers of the medium-size carnivores such as cats and foxes and it becomes essential for man to intervene. Plenty of food and good climatic conditions produce a vigorous breeding pattern, which in turn produces a higher density of animals and a greater strain on the food supply. Culling to keep the number of animals to a level that suits the existing food supply can only be good for the species.

I compared the photographs of the Revack cat with the Kellas animal before me. There was a certain resemblance: they were of similar size, both were thick coated and black with wire-like whiskers and prominent teeth. They had to be connected, despite the distance between their respective assassinations.

'What do you think?' I asked Merrily. She shook her head.

'I just don't know. It's smaller than I expected, but still it's quite a monster.' She gazed admiringly at the silently growling cat. 'He's quite spectacular, isn't he?'

I asked Tomas Christie if we could take his specimen south for examination and he agreed without hesitation.

'As long as I get it back and you look after it.'

When we arrived back in London, I had to continue on to Devon by British Rail, clutching the massive chunk of wood covered by a huge black dustbin bag through which the odd razor-sharp claw managed to hook, frequently drawing blood as if in revenge for its undignified mode of travel. The train was crowded and the guard kept pointing out that everyone would be better off if I deposited my 'parcel' in the luggage van. There was no way I was going to be parted from the stuffed cat; I offered to go with it but was told that was against the rules, so regardless of my or the other passengers' comfort I sat tight and hung on to my bit of tree and vicious plastic bag, ignoring the withering looks I was getting from other travellers.

Next day I telephoned Charles Thomas and arranged to take the specimen down to him in Cornwall. This time British Rail was not involved, although after installing it on the back seat of my car, I took the precaution of covering the cat with a sheet. The cat itself was not too cumbersome but the piece of wood to which it was wired was extremely large, heavy and awkwardly shaped. Without a cover I could not avoid the cat peering out of the window with a glassy if indignant glare.

Professor Thomas was intrigued by the Kellas specimen and suggested that we should show it to a friend of his, the retired zoologist Dr Frank Turk.

Dr Turk examined the animal carefully, snipping off the odd hair and making detailed measurements, before giving his verdict.

'I can't see any evidence of hybridization in the coat,' he announced. 'I'll have to examine it in more detail. It is a truly fascinating specimen.'

I watched these two learned men studying the strange cat

and felt relieved. Neither had sighed and dismissed the creature as simply a big moggie. I left the Kellas cat with Dr Turk and returned home to Torquay with a light heart. I had done my bit, and now the scientists could take over. It could be only a matter of time before we knew the origins of the Morayshire mystery cat.

2

A Living Legend

The difficulty of species identification from one specimen is easy to understand. The specimen could be either a hybrid of two other species, possessing features of both parents, or else simply a mutant or deformed specimen of one species. The confusion can best be illustrated by the variety of breeds of dogs, many of which would superficially appear to bear no relationship to each other. If a Great Dane is placed beside a Pekinese dog, it is hard to comprehend that both animals are of the same species. The size, skull shape and coat are all very different, yet they both belong to the species *Canis familiaris*. Despite the diverse outward appearances, the two animals contain the same genetic make-up and it is only man's interference with breeding, together with nature's ability to adapt to changing conditions, that has resulted in the external changes that confuse us.

That such changes can occur over a relatively short period can be seen in the domestic cat world. In the early years of the twentieth century two farm cats, one in Devon and one in Cornwall, produced similar unconnected deformed litters. The kittens were all born with tight curly coats. These animals were so attractive that they were subjected to intensive and careful breeding which resulted in the now accepted Devon and Cornish Rex breeds. Two identifiable breeds, apparently unlike the parent breed, were produced in less than a hundred years, nature and man combining forces to confuse the identification of the species.

In addition to such difficulties, identification of the Kellas specimen was hampered by the cat having been preserved by a taxidermist, so making impossible any genetic work at that early stage of the comparatively new scientific field. For genetic comparison the laboratory needed soft tissue and blood, both of which are absent from a stuffed specimen. Overall appearances can be deceptive too, for the parts of the animal that remain can be stretched, shrunk or otherwise distorted by the preserving processes and the skill of the taxidermist.

With all these factors taken into consideration, as well as the natural reticence of scientists to accept the possibility of anything new being discovered, I knew that identification of the Kellas cat would not come overnight. All the same, I was unprepared for the scientific scrap that lay ahead. The controversy over the existence of the British big cat was understandable: some eyewitness accounts, a few hazy photographs and a quantity of dead sheep added up to a case of circumstantial rather than actual evidence. Time and time again I was told that if only I could produce the actual body of a big cat I would be home and dry. Now that I had one body of a smaller unidentified cat I thought that I was at least halfway home.

Obviously examination was limited. Dr Turk did the best he could with the taxidermist's specimen, analysing hair and combing the coat for his particular interest – a species of mite. Part of his scientific life had been devoted to the study of the tiny mites that can be found on all living creatures and which, unlike lice and fleas that can be picked up casually by one animal from another, are passed on from mother to young at birth. The theory is that every living species has its own mite species, and so examination of the mite on a piece of skin can identify the animal skin from which it has come. If the Kellas specimen carried a mite associated with a wildcat or with a domestic cat, then we would be able to identify the Morayshire cat with that species. If the animal was the result of hybrid breeding between a wildcat and a domestic feral, then it should carry both species of mites; if it was a hitherto unrecorded black pure wildcat, it would carry only the wildcat mite, and if it was simply a mutated domestic cat, then it would carry only the domestic cat mite.

After careful combing of the Kellas coat, Frank Turk wrote to tell me he had collected parasites from the specimen and these included the biting louse *Felicola subrostrata*, which is found on both wildcats and domestic cats, and a minute and obscure mite of the family *Pediculochelidae*, measuring 0.12 mm in length, which he felt was probably a new species, maybe even new genus, although it was too broken by the mounting for him to be able to describe it. The only known species of the family had been found on bees in Durban in South Africa, on a rat in Florida, and on the jungle fowl in the Phillipines. Dr Turk commented, 'I cannot guess the significance of the specimen here.'

The connection between Florida rats, Phillipines jungle fowl, Durban bees and Scottish Kellas cats seemed almost as much of a mystery as the cats themselves. We needed to do a great deal more research to be certain of his findings, Dr Turk needed fresh specimens. According to Tomas Christie, the cat was not a one-off but one of a type seen, if not frequently, certainly on a number of occasions. If he was right, then sooner or later another Kellas had to turn up on a Morayshire estate and we had to attempt to organise things so that the next body was not destroyed or sent to the taxidermist but placed immediately in a freezer and kept for future scientific examination.

Media coverage can have its disadvantages but it also has its uses, and was just what we needed to spread the message, although I was at pains to point out that we did not want anyone killing one of the cats simply to provide us with a body. Whatever their origin, the cats were certainly rare, and I did not wish to be responsible for their extinction.

The next step was to take the stuffed Kellas to London to be examined within the hallowed halls of the British Museum of Natural History. I felt awed at the thought. By taking my evidence to the greatest natural history authority in the land I would be treading on the heels of such august figures as Charles Darwin.

While staying a couple of days at a London hostel, I found that other guests had followed the media reports about the mystery cats and I left the Kellas specimen on display in the dining room so that it could be seen by anyone interested. At breakfast on the first morning, as the stuffed cat stood glowering from his wooden stand on the sideboard, I was amused to see the hostel's pet domestic cat, a female, come hurtling into the room on her usual scrounge, and skid to an abrupt halt upon spotting the Kellas cat. She stared at the stuffed feline in horror, dropped to her belly and slowly crawled backwards for the exit, her eyes wide in disbelief. There she paused, obviously considering that behind the door represented comparative safety, and peeped round to gaze at the ferocious visitor. Gradually she gained courage and slunk back into the room, using every available bit of cover, her eyes never leaving the silently snarling specimen. Finally she summoned up enough courage to leap on to the sideboard to inspect the intruder, cautiously she sniffed the piece of wood and then sniffed the cat itself. Next she did the altogether unexpected thing and rolled at his feet. Frantically she rubbed herself against him, positively throwing herself at the handsome stranger. Passion overcame her shyness. She tried to wash his face, pressing her cheek against his unresponsive bristly jaw, purring loudly. She was in love! She became possessed with desire, sniffing his tail, rearing up against his furry flanks and blatantly lifting her tail invitingly under his rigidly snarling nose. It was a pathetic sight, this matronly feline spinster offering her all to the unresponsive super cat.

She seemed to have no suspicion that the male cat which so excited her was just a shell, no longer capable of enjoying the natural pleasures of life. It was also interesting that she should react in such a way to the Kellas: did it mean that the stuffed cat, despite its appearance, was related to the domestic cat, or would the female cat have reacted in the same way to any feline species of similar size?

I promised myself that later I would try a series of experiments to see the behaviour of domestic cats when introduced to stuffed specimens of other species of the smaller cats, such as the Scottish wildcat, the jungle cat and the leopard cat. Would they always acknowledge the more powerful species as their superior or was the conduct of the hotel cat indicative of species relationship with the Kellas? I was surprised that the living cat did not consider the other cat as just an object rather than a living creature, for surely scent should play an important part in species recognition. With no living tissue and the skin tanned and treated during the process of taxidermy, it was hard to believe the Kellas specimen still smelt like a lusty tom cat. Whatever the reason, it was certain that the Kellas had at least one ardent admirer.

When I arrived at the Natural History Museum, the doorman informed me that I couldn't take my parcel in at the front entrance, so off I trudged to the rear of the huge building, lugging the heavy chunk of wood with its vicious-clawed passenger. It was a long walk. The back entrance to the museum has nothing of the charm and architectural elegance of the front facade; rather it resembles a hybrid between a Victorian prison and a factory warehouse. I entered through the wide open large bay doors and explained that I had an appointment. It was almost an hour before Daphne Hills arrived and introduced herself. She was small, slightly built and younger than I had expected. She spoke in a slightly aloof and unfriendly manner.

'This is the Scottish cat I presume. When do you want it back?'

I told her I would be in London for only two days.

'Fine,' she said briskly. 'It'll be here at the door, waiting for you. Now you must excuse me, I'm very busy.'

I was dismissed.

On Wednesday morning I arrived with Merrily to collect the Kellas, prepared this time for the cool arm's-length response. The specimen was not awaiting me as arranged. Instead Daphne Hills appeared, beaming.

'We've had a good look at your cat,' she said. 'Come upstairs and I'll show you what we've done.'

I could hardly believe the change of attitude. She was relaxed and friendly as she led the way along countless corridors and through massive dark wood-panelled rooms lined with huge mahogany cupboards and shelves from floor to ceiling stacked with books, papers, skulls, fossils and stuffed birds and animals. It was the beating heart of the old museum, cluttered with specimens and dusty with the accumulation of years of moulting fur and feathers and disintegrating manuscripts. We reached her office where the Kellas stood snarling in isolated splendour on a table.

'He's a magnificent beast, isn't he?' she said brightly. 'A marvellous specimen of a hybrid between a Scottish wildcat and a domestic. Of course, we've always known they hybridize, but I think this must be one of best examples.'

She gazed admiringly at the snarling cat.

'But Professor Thomas and Dr Turk didn't think he could be a hybrid,' I exclaimed.

'I'm not surprised,' Miss Hills said. 'Neither did I at first. We thought he might be the first recorded melanistic wildcat, but on closer examination I'm quite sure he is a hybrid.'

'But how does that explain the others?' I asked, producing the pictures of the Revack cat. 'Here is another one.' I offered her the photographs to look at. She returned them to me after the briefest glance.

'Oh, I'm afraid we can't consider looking at pictures,' she said with a touch of her earlier haughtiness. 'We can only consider actual taxonomic evidence.'

'But the keepers and landowners in the area claim to have been killing these cats for years,' I insisted.

She shrugged. 'I'm sure they do,' she said with a quick

smile. 'They will kill a number of domestic feral cats on their land, and there's a lot of evidence to suggest that ferals can become quite large. As black is a dominant gene, I imagine black is a very common colour to find among the ferals.' She looked at the Kellas cat. 'There may be others around like him, of course but I expect most of the animals reported aren't actual hybrids but simply large melanistic ferals.'

Her tone was patronizing.

'What if they are identical to the Kellas specimen as claimed?' I inquired.

'Then I should be very interested to see them,' she said. 'With this specimen we haven't got the soft parts and the skin can easily have become distorted and stretched during the process of taxidermy. We could tell a great deal more from a fresh specimen than from this one. Well, I must get on with some work. Thank you for bringing him in to show us. He is, as I say, a superb example of a hybrid.'

It was obvious that the interview was at an end.

I was disappointed that the museum wouldn't take into consideration the existence of the Revack cat from the photographs but I still had hope that the body had survived in deep freeze somewhere. I was also convinced that Tomas Christie had not been killing large feral domestic black cats over the years.

I could understand the museum's caution and accepted that the Kellas cat might have become distorted during the mounting process. I felt certain that it would not be too long before I could produce another specimen, complete with unstretched skin and all the soft parts.

In the following April the call came. Gamekeeper Leslie Mallinson, who was working at Advie, not far from Aviemore in the Grampian mountains, had killed a strange large black cat and a local policeman had suggested that I might be interested in the animal. He said he had put the carcase in the freezer, and as he was now coming to Devon to visit friends, he could deliver the body if I wanted it. I assured him that I did.

The Advie cat was still half-frozen when I met Leslie in a Torquay car park. As soon as he lifted the black dustbin bag from the back of his car, I knew without a doubt it was a cat like the Kellas specimen. The size and the long-legged, long-bodied lean shape was unmistakeable. I had at last got a complete body, with all its soft parts to take intact to the museum! I telephoned the museum immediately.

To say they were not interested would be an understatement. They refused even to consider looking at the carcase unless I was willing to pay for the privilege of them doing so. Finally, after a good deal of argument, I was told that, if I were willing to present them with the animal as a gift, they would examine it without charge.

I was unhappy with the whole situation. I had intended to give them the animal anyway, but I did not like the pressure being put on me. It seemed to me like a form of blackmail, forcing me to give them the animal or else they would not even admit it existed.

I agreed to their demands under duress and informed Andrew Barker, a friend and an independent television producer, that I would be travelling to London with the Advie cat if he and his colleagues would like to see it. He asked me to bring the Kellas as well and made arrangements to film the two animals before I handed over the Advie cat to the British Museum of Natural History. I was unsure what would become of the specimen once I had parted with it, and felt that if I never saw it again, at least there would be some record on film of the animal.

Andrew arranged for his camera crew to meet me off the train and whisk me away for filming the cats during a veterinary examination before taking the Advie cat to the Kensington museum the following morning. They would then film me entering the museum, and Andrew wanted to accompany me inside the building to see for himself precisely what took place.

The vet was filmed while he measured the Advie cat, examining its teeth to estimate its age and x-raying the skull.

Then the two cats were again subjected to the intense heat of floodlights as they underwent a further photographic session during which the Kellas specimen remained unruffled by all the attention while the Advie cat, now at melting point, leaked pools of watery blood on to the carpet.

The following morning we took the fully thawed cat to the museum, anxious to hear what they had to say about it. This time I went directly to the back door, accompanied by Andrew. We were taken upstairs to meet Daphne Hills' boss, Ian Bishop. Introductions were made and I began to unwrap the limp body of the Advie cat. Abruptly I was stopped by Mr Bishop.

'I'm sorry,' he said. 'You can't unwrap that now.'

I was confused. 'Why not?'

'I'm sorry, but I'm afraid it's against the rules. We cannot examine the animal with you present.'

I had lugged the dead body in a suitcase on a train from Devon to London and they were calmly informing me that the wrapping wasn't to be removed in my presence. It made no sense.

'But I just wanted Miss Hills to see if she agreed it was the same as the Kellas cat.'

He shook his head. 'I simply cannot allow it to be opened with a member of the public present.'

I changed the subject to the history of the cat. After a few minutes' conversation I said, 'I'm afraid the exit wound is a bit of a mess, I hope it doesn't affect your preserving of the specimen. See?'

Before anyone could stop me I had whipped the cat literally out of the bag.

Daphne Hills stared at the Advie cat. 'It's very like the other one,' she agreed.

I was satisfied.

Bishop promised me a copy of the report as soon as it was completed and then Andrew and I were escorted from the building. Though it was polite behaviour, I could not escape from the impression that they wanted to be absolutely sure we had finally left the premises.

As we walked out of the building, Andrew turned towards me with a mixture of shock and admiration on his face.

'Di,' he said in hushed tones. 'You manipulated that man!'

I agreed without conscience. I had wanted to see the surprised expressions on their faces when they saw the Kellas cat's twin – the cat that is now registered as BM(NH) 85.81.5 in the museum's collection.

Back at home I eargerly anticipated the museum's report on the Advie specimen. It turned into a long wait.

Meanwhile, on 14th October, a juvenile male Kellas cat was killed at Kellas and examined by a Forres veterinary surgeon, John Robertson, who took a sample of blood and forwarded it to the Department of Zoology at the University of Aberdeen for genetic analysis. Unfortunately the blood was delivered to the wrong department, where it remained untraced for twenty-four hours, the delay making the specimen useless for study. The failure of the blood culture of the third Kellas specimen only emphasised the problem of carrying out genetic work on carcases where there was a lengthy delay between the death of the animal and the arrival of the specimen in scientific hands.

The obvious answer was to capture a live specimen and take a blood sample from it without causing the animal any harm. Unfortunately gamekeepers normally don't trap them alive, and with so many different estates in such a vast area, it was an impossible task to persuade every gamekeeper to change his methods of working. I had to be content with choosing the Forres area where both Tomas Christie's estate and the nearby Darnaway Estate, the traditional seat of the Earl of Moray, were situated. As in so many professions, gamekeepers are very much a social clique who co-operate with their neighbours. A roving hungry fox will not stop at estate boundaries. I hoped that word of mouth would ensure that, if there were the possibility of catching a live Kellas, then we had a better than even chance of getting it.

There were other avenues of research to follow while I waited for the museum report. It is well known that native tales and legend can often carry a root of truth beneath the fanciful outer coating. Such species as the gorilla, the okapi and the Komodo dragon were native legends that eventually became fact instead of folklore. A more recent discovery was made by John Blashford-Snell in 1979 on an expedition during which the team heard about Atrellia, a giant tree-climbing crocodile that breathed fire. Intrigued by the story, they set about searching for the fanciful creature only to discover a monstrous form of Salvador's monitor, the size of a crocodile with dark green skin, a red mouth from which the flickering reptile's tongue appeared to the frightened natives as flames. I wondered if there were any cat legends in the areas where the Kellas cats were being found.

According to *Superstitions of the Highlands and Islands of Scotland* by J. G. Campbell, published in 1900, there had existed Cait Sith, a shape-changing witch who haunted the Highlands in the form of a fairy cat. The Highland Fairy Cat was said to be extremely ferocious, the size of a small dog, jet black in colour with large fangs and a white star or spot on its chest. As if this description were not already enough to terrify the unwary traveller, it was further enhanced by Cait Sith being described as always seen surrounded by a halo of sparks, or stars. It was not hard to imagine the effect of encountering a dog-size snarling black cat in the darkness of the forest, surrounded by a luminous glow of shimmering stars.

No one had suspected that the fairy cat could have been a living animal because of the halo of stars, yet it was that very description that excited me. The Kellas cat, although small, was certainly much larger than the average domestic cat, and was indeed the size of a small dog. It was jet black with a median thoracic white spot or white star on its chest. It had larger than normal very noticeable white teeth. All in all, the flesh and blood Kellas cat could be described in almost exactly the same terms as of the legendary fairy cat. Except, of course, for the impossible halo of sparks or stars. Yet one of the striking features of the Kellas cats were the long coarse white guard hairs sprinkled throughout the coat, especially across the flanks and hind quarters.

I placed the mounted Kellas specimen in the corner of a dark room and shone a torch beam on to the shadowy animal. As the light played across the snarling creature, the white teeth shone ominiously, lending its expression added ferocity, and the white guard hairs scattered throughout the coat shone with a brilliant reflected light. The animal was suddenly surrounded by a halo of shimmering stars. A legend was suddenly taking solid form before me. A legend come to life!

Was I meeting Cait Sith in the partial flesh?

It was easy to understand the description that had seemed so unreal before. The cat, encountered suddenly in the darkness of the forest, its back arched, its fur erect in fear and aggression, snarling in anger at the disturbance, lit only by the moon or the flickering light beam from a lamp, could certainly appear like Cait Sith. No wonder it had terrified superstitious travellers. And if the legend was describing the Kellas cats, then they had been around for hundreds of years – hardly a sudden freak of genetic mutation or resulting from a recent hybrid mating.

If the Natural History Museum staff would not look at a photograph of a specimen that had been measured and examined at the time of its death, they certainly weren't going to take into consideration a six-hundred year old folk tale. Science itself would have to provide proof of the creature's long term existence.

Dr Turk suggested that science might be able to do that by comparing the Kellas cats with another felid that had been discovered nearly a hundred years earlier. On examining the first Kellas specimen, he had remarked on the similarities to Satunin's cat, a black form of wildcat described in the 'Proceedings of the Zoological Society of London, vol 11' in 1904. The eminent Russian zoologist, C. Satunin, had been studying the wildcats of Transcaucasia and described specimens of what he believed was a new species of black wildcat.

Although the existence in Transcaucaucasia of a black wildcat was known long ago, the animal has never been described or scientifically named ... all the specimens I have had the opportunity of examining are alike ... I name it *Felis deamon*, of which the following is a description: – Size of a big male domestic cat ... very long white hairs, scantily dispersed over the body ... the tail is conspicuously longer than in *Felis catus*.

I agreed with Dr Turk. It does not take a lifetime of academic study to recognize the similarities between the description of Satunin's cat and the Kellas cats – except for the length of the tail, which in the case of the Kellas cat is shorter than the average wildcat (*Felis silvestris*), which in turn is considerably shorter than that of the domestic cat, and the lack of any mention of the median thoracic white spot, (also found in *Felis silvestris* as recorded by Konrad Gesner in the sixteenth century). Satunin even noted the long white guard hairs that were such a feature of the Kellas cats.

Satunin's report, however, was dismissed by later scientists. In 1935 the specimens he had collected were re-examined by others who decided they were nothing more than the results of hybrid breeding between wildcats and domestic cats. Satunin's original findings were promptly dismissed and *Felis daemon* was demoted.

A great deal of research is being carried out at present to determine just how much interbreeding has occured between *Felis silvestris* and the vast population of feral domestic cats across Europe, with particular interest in Britain because of its island division from the mainland mass. The wildcat, once common across the whole of the British Isles, is now only found in the wild country in the north of Scotland and its official title of *Felis silvestris grampia* records its last stronghold against the ravages of man – the Grampian mountain range in the north-east Highlands.

The species was verging on extinction in the early twentieth century and only began to make a comeback when the 1914–18 war took so many young men from their homeland and rural occupations to fight and die in the muddy trenches of

European battlefields. The Highlands of Scotland were suddenly stripped of the gamekeepers, gillies, underkeepers and even poachers that kept the wild predators in check, and most of these men never returned to their former rural occupations, leaving the huge estates undermanned and the wildlife flourishing.

The land lying fallow then attracted massive forestry plantings. Hundreds of square miles of dark, closely-growing trees remained undisturbed for thirty to forty years, providing ideal breeding grounds for the shy and secretive wildcat.

The conditions were also suitable for a large increase in the numbers of feral domestic cats and semi-feral farm cats which had been kept in check when the land was extensively keepered. So the true wildcat and the imported domestic feral, which originated in Egypt and possibly arrived in Britain with the Romans, have thrived and increased in numbers over the past eighty years in the north of Scotland. Some fear, however, that the vast number of feral domestic cats could be interbreeding with the pure wildcats and so diluting the native species.

Many scientists, while willing to accept that hybridization between the two species does occur, do not believe it poses a serious threat to the native species, but others are convinced that the interbreeding occurs on such a large scale that genetic dillution must be the inevitable outcome. With more than a thousand years of both cat species sharing this small island, could the truth be that there are no longer any pure bred wildcats left? It is a strong argument in support of those who dismiss the Kellas cats as nothing more than the result of interbreeding between the two species.

Only research in the comparatively new field of genetics can provide more information. Satunin's discovery might have been dismissed in 1935 on simple personal judgement, one scientist's opinion against another's, but in future it is to be hoped that only detached impersonal scientific evidence will provide the answers. A programme of trapping, tagging and taking blood samples from wildcats in the Highlands is at present being undertaken by Scottish Natural Heritage in order to monitor numbers and range, and attempt to determine the extent of hybridization between the species. It is possible that, rather than thriving, the pure wildcat should be taken from the endangered list and added to the long list of extinctions.

Hybridization would be an easy explanation to account for both Satunin's black cat and for the Kellas specimens, but was it correct?

One of Satunin's specimens is in the British Museum, and when I collected the mounted Kellas from Daphne Hills, I asked if she considered the Scottish black cat could have any relationship with *Felis daemon*? She showed me the skin of the Satunin's cat and assured me that it was highly unlikely. The specimen skin was softly tanned, stitched and stuffed into a sausage shape, with ears, dangling paws and a tail. It is the scientific equivalent of a draught excluder and unlike a mounted taxidermist's specimen does not show the overall shape and external appearance of the original animal.

The Transcaucasian specimen appeared to be a much smaller animal than the Kellas cats, difficult as it was to compare the two animals. The coat texture was soft and thick, very like the Scottish specimens, but the overall colour was a dark chocolate with reddish brown overtones rather than the true black of the Kellas. None the less, the brown was of a similar coloration to the shading on the jaw and inside the legs that gave the Kellas cats a slight russet tinge. I wondered if the Russian cat had been darker when it was first killed and had faded over the long years exposed to light. The long coarse white guard hairs, however, were common to both cats. If the two were not identical, there were definite similarities. Different habitat and climatic variations could perhaps account for minor changes within the species. Athough there is no conclusive proof to date that the Kellas cats and Satunin's cats are related, it remains a distinct possibility.

I had kept the mounted Kellas cat for more than a year and it was time to return it to Tomas Christie. We had all the information that the specimen could provide. Months passed before I heard any word of the promised report from the museum. The only consolation I had was that Thomas and a number of the gamekeepers on adjoining estates in the northeast of Scotland were certain that the Advie cat was the first of many specimens I would receive. There was already the young male killed at Kellas waiting for me in the freezer, so I decided to return to Scotland to hand the mounted specimen back to Tomas and to collect the frozen one that I was determined would not go to the South Kensington museum.

I stayed with Tomas and his wife for a few days, exploring the countryside and meeting some of the people living in the area. I was hoping to meet John Doune, whose newspaper cutting had started the whole hunt for the smaller mystery cats, but unfortunately he was away in Australia. His parents, Lord and Lady Moray, invited me to dinner so that I could meet the family, and I took with me to Darnaway Castle the mounted specimen of Tomas's Kellas cat.

The castle, which is open to the public during the summer months, is situated deep in forestry land a few miles from Forres. Part of it dates from the fifteenth century but the building has been redesigned and enlarged in classical style, in 1802, resulting in an imposing Georgian residence hidden from the modern world by its sheltering thicket of dark and gloomy trees, the remains of a once vast ancient forest that protected the former Earls of Moray in more bloodthirsty and violent times.

I parked in the drive in front of impressive stone steps that were guarded by lines of heraldic stone beasts. The sun was sinking, touching the building and the surrounding tree tops with a golden rosy glow that added to the timeless feel of the landscape. I walked slowly up the steps, enjoying the view, and then found it wasn't only the forest that protected the Earls of Moray from disturbance, Nothing resembling a working doorbell could I find.

I retreated, looking for a side door or some sign of human activity. The setting sun turned the windows to sheets of molten gold but the magic mood was gone, I was now worried about my late arrival, or rather my late entrance. Luckily, just as I was wondering whether to give up and go home, a sports car came hurtling down the drive, another dinner guest arriving. As a frequent visitor to the castle, he showed me how to gain entrance.

You just opened the glass door, walked into the Great Hall and in a loud voice, shouted "Hoi, we're here!"

I would never have thought of that!

Later that evening, I took the Kellas cat into the castle and displayed him in the drawing room. We turned out the lights, and by the light of the flickering log fire and a torch beam, I recounted the story of the Highland Fairy Cat while the Kellas snarled in the darkness, its teeth and star glowing eerily and its white guard hairs displaying its shimmering halo. It was a fitting setting for the Fairy Cat to make its reappearance in the Scottish Highlands.

All too soon it was time to be heading back south. I made a sudden decision. To continue the research on the Kellas cats, I was going to be faced with frequent commuting between Devon and Morayshire, no small distance, and when in Forres I spotted a derelict cottage for sale in a solicitor's window, there and then I decided to buy it.

I was still carrying on the search to identify the British Big Cat, and as the Forres area was the centre of sightings of both the leopard-size and the Kellas mystery cats it made sense to go where I could best carry on my study of both species.

I had fallen in love with the slower pace of life in the north and the beautiful landscape – the land of the red deer and purple heather, where the scent of pine trees mingled with smoke from the peat fires. In the village of Dallas, near Kellas, I would be living on the edge of the last great wilderness of Britain, in the world of the Kellas cats.

3

Shock Waves

The new Kellas cat, a young male about eleven months old, was lighter in weight than the Advie cat but it had the same accentuated long, lean and leggy appearance and identical black coat colour with the white chest and belly patches and the same long white guard hairs scattered throughout its fur.

The Darnaway gamekeeper also snared a similar black female cat but this was shorter in the leg and of a slightly stockier build. I collected that carcase on my next trip to Scotland when I was negotiating the purchase of the cottage. If it hadn't been for the coat and small head I might have dismissed the Darnaway cat as a domestic feral. It certainly wasn't identical to the males but it carried enough similar characteristics to identify it as being related to them. Was this the first sign of dilution of a hybrid? If so, it still provided no proof of the theory that the Kellas cats were merely hybrids of domestics and wildcats.

Dilution certainly appeared to be present, but dilution of what? Domestic cat/wildcat, or domestic cat/Kellas cat, or even wildcat/ Kellas cat?

At last the British Museum released the long awaited report on the Advie cat. This was no longer of importance to me as I already knew its basic conclusions – a probable hybrid – but I was curious to see the evidence by which the official conclusion was reached. I had made a special request for the coat to be examined for species mite, to see if Dr Turk's findings could be verified. I didn't have a lot of faith that the museum study would go much beyond a cursory external examination and an internal weight and measurement programme, so I decided to consult an independent scientist who was involved in genetic research. Professor Berry of London University, an expert in this exciting new field, agreed to give laboratory time to attempting to identify the species to which the Kellas cats belonged, although he warned me of the obstacles to be overcome and said that he could not guarantee a successful outcome, much depending on the freshness of the specimens provided. As the science advanced and improved its techniques, it would become easier to extract the DNA from specimens for the purpose of building up their genetic pattern. To identify a species by its genetic pattern, that pattern has to have been recorded already for comparision to be made. Unfortunately no work had been done on any cat species, added to which all cat species are so closely related – and that is why the different species can so readily interbreed – that the differences in the genetic pattern will be slight.

I agreed to deliver the two new specimens, the young male Kellas and the Darnaway female to his laboratory so that the internal organs could be removed and used to extract the DNA, and at the same time I decided to call on Daphne Hills at the Natural History Museum, to show her the new bodies and collect the Advie cat report in person.

John Doune, now home from Australia and studying at London University, was also eager to see for the first time the animals that he had been instrumental in bringing to everyone's notice, and he and Andrew Barker joined me at Merrily's home for dinner with two extra guests who would not be needing places at table. There must be few dinner parties where the guests of honour are two dead cats.

The following morning we arrived at the museum and parked in the rear car park, leaving the Kellas carcases in the car boot. Daphne Hills met us and handed me a copy of the official report on the Advie cat, apologising for the long delay. From a glance, the report held no surprises, but I was shocked by the footnote on the final page that expressly forbade me to publish the findings in any form or to release them to the media. In effect, the museum had forced me to present them with the cat that I had gone to considerable expense to find and was now banning me from using the results of my own efforts. No reason was given for this censorship. I was simply gagged!

I wondered whether the ban would hold up in court. Had the Advie cat been the only specimen, such behaviour by the establishment would have caused dreadful problems, but as I had two more bodies, I could afford to shrug off their attempts to block the research.

The whole episode left a nasty taste. I was reminded of the opposition to Darwin when he dared to suggest that the origins of man had been by evolution from an ape-like primitive ancestor rather than the Biblical dividing up Adam to make Eve. Such bigotry was shocking but perhaps understandable in the rigid Victorian period, but that such establishment prejudice as Darwin encountered should still flourish in the age of technology in the twentieth century was to me profoundly disturbing.

I had some sympathy for Daphne Hills, for although she was part of the system, I felt she was an unwilling part. Others before her had also been faced with the decision of staying with the system and trying to do their work despite it, or of rebelling and finding themselves on the outside looking in. The establishment has the power and the individual thinker has very little chance to fight on its ground.

I asked Daphne Hills if she would like to see the two new Kellas specimens. She was very interested, and we went down to the car park where I opened the boot and tipped the two defrosting carcases out of their plastic bags on to the tarmac. She stood looking at the two limp bedraggled cats, their fur lank and wet, their eyes blank and cloudy, their lips pulled back in a last snarl, revealing their white canines protruding from bloodless gums. Even death could not disguise the size, the long lean shape of the animals and the length of leg.

'They are very like the others,' she said softly. It was all she could say.

Professor Berry was away but his staff were friendly and helpful and interested in the challenge of identifying the strange cats. They explained the uncertainties of the process involved and the slim chance there was of success using frozen carcases, but they agreed to do their best with the material provided and I, in turn, agreed to try and obtain fresher specimens or, if possible, to trap a live cat. To catch a live Kellas and sedate it so that a sample of fresh blood could be taken before its release back into the wild was of course the ideal, but I could not expect to achieve that on my own, without the co-operation of landowners and estate workers. It was just a matter of time before a Kellas found itself in a humane walk-in trap somewhere rather than caught with a wire noose wrapped tightly around its neck.

Professor Berry's team removed the organs they needed from the two cats and returned the bodies to me to be replaced in deep freeze before being passed on to a taxidermist. I had done all I could in London. It was time for me to return to Torquay, put my home up for sale, and move to Scotland.

If I accepted that I did not have the facilities for the capture of a live Kellas, there were others who did, and among these were the producers of the BBC television science series *Tomorrow's World*. I first heard about their activities when I received a rather embarrassed phone call from Tomas Christie at Kellas.

'I'm sworn to secrecy but I thought you ought to know that a TV camera team has been working up here for the past few weeks and yesterday they caught a live Kellas!'

I was shocked and excited – shocked because I had known nothing about it, but excited because the existence of the trapped Kellas would provide the fresh blood specimen for the genetic research. After all my efforts to prove that the animal was worth studying, I felt hurt at discovering the whole operation being carried on behind my back. If it had not been for Tomas feeling pangs of conscience, I would have known nothing about the animal being trapped until it became public knowledge.

Despite my personal feeling of rejection, I decided to contact the BBC as the importance of obtaining a blood sample for the genetic research far outweighed any damage to my ego. I rang the *Tomorrow's World* office, explained my involvement with the cats and requested confirmation of the capture of the live Kellas. I asked if a blood sample could be forwarded to Professor Berry. I was told politely that my request would be passed on. A few days later I received a phone call from an assistant producer of the programme.

'Hello Di, my name is Martin Hughes-Games, Hughes as in Howard and Games as in Olympica.'

He confirmed that they had indeed trapped a female black wild cat at Kellas and that it was now in captivity in the Highland Wildlife Park at Kincraig.

'If you happen to be in Scotland during the next few weeks, perhaps you would call in at the park and have a look at our cat,' he suggested smugly. He then dropped the bombshell. 'I was going to give you a call some time as you're mentioned in the report on the Advie cat which we got from the British Museum.'

It appeared that just four days after I had been given the long awaited report on the Advie cat, with its restriction on publishing the results in any form, the Natural History Museum had sold its contents to the *Tomorrow's World* production team to use as they wished. I decided that I would never again deal with the British Museum of Natural History whatever information or specimens I obtained in the future.

As I was going to be in Scotland within a few days to confirm the purchase of the Dallas cottage, I phoned the wildlife park to arrange to see the cat. I knew that Eddie Orbell, the park manager, had previously examined the Revack cat killed by Ronnie Douglas, and had actually taken the photographs of the carcase that Ronnie sent me. I asked him about the *Tomorrow's World* cat, but he was not very enthusiastic.

'Can't see what the fuss is about,' he told me. 'It looks just like an ordinary moggie to me.'

'It's not the same as the Revack cat then?' I asked.

'Not to me, it isn't. That cat was a monster, this one is just the size of your average domestic moggie. Still, come and have a look at it for yourself.'

I thanked him and put down the phone thoughtfully. Had the BBC team really caught the first live Kellas or had they merely trapped a domestic cat? I called Tomas, and he confirmed that the cat was a lot smaller than the other specimens. He too was uncertain as to whether the trapped animal was indeed a pure Kellas. The colour was right, the black coat with the startling white guard hairs, but the huge size and the long-legged rangy build was not in evidence. I was suddenly not so sure that the *Tomorrow's World* team had been as clever as they thought.

Although spring had arrived in Devon, the yellow daffodils and creamy primroses reflecting the watery sun in banks and drifts along the road verges, the long drive north took me back into winter. The Scottish mountains were still snow-capped, the lower slopes streaked with blackened heather stalks and rusty dead bracken fronds. The park was closed to visitors when I arrived, the car park deserted and the barriers down. I found a track leading from a side road up through the deer enclosures to a wooded area beyond which I could see the cluster of huts and buildings of the park offices. I drove up and parked as Eddie Orbell came out to meet me. He told me that the black cat was not accepting her captivity and never showed herself during daylight hours, remaining huddled in the back of her sleeping box, avoiding all contact with humans.

'I'm afraid there's not much hope of you seeing her,' he said cheerfully. 'We can tip her out of the box if you insist,' he added. 'That's what the television crew did in order to film her. She went absolutely berserk, throwing herself at the wire in panic. I wasn't at all happy about it, seeing the animal so distressed. I'd rather not have to do it to her again as she's having difficulty adjusting.'

I agreed with him. However much I wanted to see the cat I did not want to cause the poor beast any unnecessary stress. We walked across to a nearby row of small netted enclosures which formed the isolation block where animals were kept away from the public. New arrivals remained here until they had accepted their new surroundings and become familar with the keepers. It was also used for nervous, sick or even breeding animals, the pens being so close to the office block that it was easy to keep a constant eye on the animals at risk.

The *Tomorrow's World* cat was in a pen next to a particularly large Scottish wildcat that lay draped comfortably across a vine-screened shelf, gazing out at our approach with malevolent golden eyes. He snarled lazily, a token objection to our presence, stretched his powerful body languidly and scratched the shelf with razor sharp-claws.

'He's a beauty,' I said.

The park manager nodded. 'Isn't he? He's the biggest wildcat I've ever seen. A beautiful specimen.'

And he certainly was. His short thick legs ended in large paws that dangled over the edge of the shelf, his heavy striped body sprawled, his huge head, the broad forehead marked with the distinctive M lifted, his small ears flattened to the side of his head, so unlike the upright pricked alert ears of the domestic cat. Yet, although of record size, he was quite unlike the tall slim build of the Kellas cats.

If the true wildcat was willing to be viewed, the same could not be said of the 'Tomorrow's World' cat. The wildcat's neighbouring pen appeared to be empty of anything living. The manager pointed towards a timber barrel lying on its side in the fairly lush vegetation.

'She's in her sleeping quarters as usual. The only way of seeing her will be to go into the enclosure and crouch down to peer in, I'm afraid.'

It certainly wasn't what I would have wished, but it looked as if that was the only view I was going to get. I nodded.

'You won't see much,' he added, unlocking the gate and leading the way into the tiny pen. I followed nervously.

Sinking down on my haunches and bending my head. I peered into the gloomy interior of the small barrel. At once I was greeted with a low throbbing growl, to be followed by a short loud spit.

In the dim light that filtered through the tiny entrance I could at first see only the heaped bedding straw, then I could make out a low dark shape at the rear of the barrel, only the white teeth and the blazing golden eyes clearly visible.

The cat was pressed against the back of her quarters, sunk down so low that only the dark outline of her head and flattened ears could be seen. She was gleaming black, with wide round eyes of extraordinary intensity, a piercing orange colour that blazed with hatred. She spat and snarled, revealing a bright pinky red mouth and tongue against which the sharp white teeth glowed in the darkness.

I could not see her body shape, her tail or any detail of coat colour, but she was definitely only the size of a domestic cat, and not a very large one at that. She certainly wasn't Kellas size. I stood up but the spitting fury continued from the barrel even though I was no longer in vision.

'She looks small,' I said, disappointed.

'She is. Not even big for a domestic cat.'

'What length of leg has she, tall or short?'

He shrugged. 'I'd say normal for a domestic cat, quite short. Nothing like that monster at Revack.

'And her tail, is it long and slim like a domestic cat or short and clubbed like a wildcat?'

'Oh, long and slim. As I've said, she looks just like an ordinary moggie. She's just a bit wild, that's all. Possibly a hybrid between a wildcat and a domestic. She is not accepting captivity as I would expect a normal feral domestic cat to do.'

The outraged growls and snarls coming from the wooden barrel confirmed his opinion. If her family background was just of domestic origin, they must have been a pretty bad tempered lot. Even the geniune wildcat next door was looking rather shocked at the language coming from his neighbour's bedroom. It looked as if the *Tomorrow's World* cat was exactly what one would expect a domestic wildcat hybrid to be.

A couple of days after I arrived back home in Torquay, I received another phone call from Martin Hughes-Games.

'Well, have you seen our cat?' he chirruped.

'Yes.'

'And what do think of her?'

'I'm afraid I don't think she's a Kellas. She's very wild but the shape isn't right for a Kellas cat.'

There was a pause. 'Of course she's a Kellas! She's black with the white guard hairs and chest spot.' The voice was not now so patronizingly friendly.

'I'm sorry. She seems to be just a black cat, nothing like a Kellas. She is not big enough. She's half the size of a Kellas and she doesn't appear to have the tall lean shape of the Kellas. Eddie Orbell agrees with me.'

Martin Hughes-Games was no longer even slightly friendly. 'You're just saying that because you didn't catch her,' he sneered and put down the phone.

Ah, well, I thought. He'd asked for my opinion and I'd given it! He'd only got to ask Tomas Christie, Eddie Orbell, Charles Thomas, Frank Turk or Ronnie Douglas for their opinions and I knew they would all agree with me. The simple fact was that the female cat in the Highland Wildlife Park was not as large nor had the build of a Kellas. Its chief similarity appeared to be its coat colour – and some black domestic cats have white guard hairs.

I planned to move to Scotland at the beginning of April. Shortly beforehand I heard from friends on Exmoor that the *Tomorrow's World* team had been interviewing witnesses about the Exmoor beast. I wondered what possible connection could be made between the big panther-size cat and the small Scottish felid and presumed that the programme's pro-

Shock Waves

ducers had abandoned claims to have solved the Kellas mystery and were simply going to compare the nationwide sightings. I dismissed the TV programme content as of no significance to my own research.

Within a few days three dogs and a cat and I were on our way to our new home in Scotland, with the furniture van booked to follow us. The dogs – two Great Danes and a miscellaneous mutt – were fine, sleeping for most of the long journey, but the cat, Pansy, was far from happy. The P, as she was usually called, had always been temperamental, a trait she had revealed from three weeks of age when she had been rescued from drowning. Knowing her nature and the length of the journey, I had gone to my local vet for advice before the trip.

'I'll give you some tablets,' he had said, the relief of losing a certain patient obvious on his face. 'For cats I would recommend one tablet to make them sleep, given half an hour before the journey, two tablets will knock them out completely, like an anaesthetic, so you have to keep them well wrapped up and warm because they will lose body heat. A hot water bottle is a good idea.' He paused. 'For Pansy,' he added thoughtfully, 'I would definitely recommend two tablets.'

Half an hour before setting off I thrust the tablets down a protesting throat and half-throttled her until she swallowed. I checked that her mouth was empty, having had past experience of Pansy and pills. Half an hour later, when it was time to fill the hotwater bottle, the doped cat was trying out her tightroping skills along a curtain rail. An hour later we were on the road, the three undoped dogs snoring their heads off, the doped cat fighting mad, ripping her way out of the cat basket and screaming her protests. For twenty-two hours the feline protests never let up except for one brief respite when we reached Edinburgh and she lost her voice. She clung to my shoulder all sixteen claws dug in and opened her mouth pathetically miming her protests. The peace lasted for about half an hour and we finally reached Dallas with her still in full screech.

49

The cottage was semi-derelict. Half the floors were missing but it had a roof and the electricity had been put in, so I unloaded the camp bed and my sleeping bag and collapsed in a shattered heap on the few remaining bare boards. Beyond the crumbling walls, in the forests that stretched away from the tiny village, black cats hunted through the night, slipping silently through the shadows just a mile from where I slept.

During my first day in the village I was able to explore the cottage and surrounding area for the first time and to plan where I was going to store the furniture while the building was being repaired. I needn't have bothered for the long-awaited furniture van never arrived. The driver made off with the lot. Later I learned that he ended up in one of Her Majesty's hotels, though unfortunately not for the theft of all my property. He had also stolen from Newton Abbot Council a painting valued at £25,000. In order to recover the painting for the poor Council, which had forgotten of its existence in store until it was stolen, all other charges were dropped, including those involving the theft of all my worldly goods. Still at least I had the cottage even if I didn't have anything in it. I began to spend a lot of time at Scottish auctions.

Andrew Barker asked if he could come to visit me. With the lack of any physical comforts, I tried to put him off. 'It's a bit rough,' I explained.

'Oh, I don't mind,' he said cheerfully. 'I'll bring a tent.'

Just one week after my arrival, I met him off the train at nearby Forres. He was impressed by the drive out to the tiny village but was less taken with the primitive conditions in which I was living.

'Good God, when you say rough, you mean rough!' he exclaimed as he walked gingerly across the planks that substituted for a floor. I had no television set but accepted a neighbour's invitation for Andrew and I to watch the feline mystery unravelled on *Tomorrow's World*. The prescreening hype had been tremendous. The *Radio Times* included a two-page spread under the headline 'Claws', which just about said it all. The article was illustrated with a full-page colour photograph of Tomas's stuffed cat and a number of newspaper clippings about research into mystery wild cats. The clippings also constantly referred to me as carrying out the research but there was no mention of my name in the text of article. Clearly I was blacklisted.

To say that the *Tomorrow's World* team had compiled a confusing muddle of fact and fiction would be understating the fact. The programme was a mish-mash of information, wrong conclusions and false claims. It started by interviewing witnesses claiming to have seen the beast of Exmoor and discussed animals the size of lions and leopards that were capable of killing and eating full grown sheep and goats, leaving pawprints four inches across. Then it claimed proudly that the mystery beasts were a mystery no longer for *Tomorrow's World* had solved the puzzle by trapping a specimen of the unknown cats in Scotland. They showed the Advie cat's skin at the British Museum, a specimen that some unnamed person had just handed over as a curiosity, and then they produced their own black cat which, they claimed, solved the whole wildcat mystery. It was a hybrid between the domestic cat and the wildcat. A short clip was shown of the small black cat racing around her enclosure in the Highland Wildlife Park after she had been tipped out of the security of her sleeping den. More than ever I shared Eddie Orbell's indignation at the panic the poor creature suffered at such treatment.

The programme made no attempt to explain how their 'Kellas' cat, the size of a small domestic pussy, could terrorize hundreds of miles of Devon and Somerset, defeat hundreds of armed farmers, police marksmen and Royal Marine Commandos and kill and devour numerous sheep, often stripping up to seventy pounds of meat in one sitting. All in all, I considered that the programme was playing games with the credulity of the British public. I was not the only one. The *Forres Gazette* ran an article headlined 'TV Tale of the Cat No Answer'.

However ridiculous were the claims of the programme, they did cause some problems in the genuine research project. Some people, perhaps only half-watching, accepted the absurd notions the programme put across. Others who had experienced loss of livestock, or who had actually seen the big cats, were justifiably angry to be told their experiences could be put down to the predations of an ordinary small domestic cat. As a result the genuine Kellas project was almost destroyed. The months I had spent persuading gamekeepers and landowners not to shoot the black cats because of their possible importance to science were ruined. Why should these men take the trouble to interrupt their work or put their birds at risk just to preserve a domestic moggie? Far better to kill the predators, as they had been doing for years, and sling the carcase into the nearest ditch. The end of the matter.

Because it was fronted as a genuine scientifically researched programme, its audience would tend to believe its message. But viewers had not been presented with the genuine facts and I was prevented by the museum from publishing any information about the Advie cat.

After the *Tomorrow's World* screening other stories about the cats appeared in the media. The *Forres Gazette* reported seventy-seven-year-old Jock Douglas describing a history of Kellas cat sightings in generations of his family.

'Everyone in the Dallas area knows about the cat. It's the Wangye cat. It's been around for hundreds of years I suppose, generations of Dallas folk have seen it.' Mr Douglas went on, 'My grandfather had Wangye Croft and I remember asking him about the cat when I was about ten. I had seen the cat while fishing with my brother at the Park Farm Pool on the Lossie in 1920. A gamekeeper called Binnie shot the animal and came down to us and said he'd killed a "big beast", and it turned out to be what my grandfather called the Wangye cat.' He described the Wangye as being longer, slimmer and more powerful than a domestic cat or the wildcat. He said, 'They were always black, moved with a lope and grew to more than four feet long when adult size. I've seen quite a few, most of them dead after being shot by keepers, but there were also live sightings. One of the most unusual features was that they swam in the Lossie and fished, often they were mistaken for otters because of their squat black heads, but they were Wangye cats. They bothered no one.'

The report continued with Mr Douglas's colourful reminisences, tales of the shooting and trapping of various unfortunate Wangyes, five shot by a keeper called Fowler at Burnside farm between 1920 and 1924. 'Older Dallas people knew the Wangye Cat story perfectly well. They knew that when it fed it never tore its prey, it would skin birds and rabbits and always leave the heads and tails of fish.

I think there are some folk would like to think they've found something new – it's not! It's like the osprey. We were told there were none left and the public were conned into thinking the Boat of Garten one was the only one – there were lots in the area.

I think the cats are the same. Aye, they're different but they're not new. They're big, bonny looking animals and Dallas has known them as neighbours for generations. The Wangye is like an old friend.'

He also said that the 'Tomorrow's World' cat was 'more a moggie than one of the proper Dallas cats'. But he added that 'The stuffed animal Tomas Christie of Kellas has is a Wangye. That creature I saw on TV is the wrong shape, the head's different – it's just not the Dallas Wangye cat.'

I asked Tomas Christie, whose family owned the area where Wangye Croft was, about Mr Douglas's grandfather, but Tomas could tell me nothing about the family. Whether the tale of the Wangye cat was also a description of the Kellas cat, or whether it was simply a charming story told by a delightful old raconteur, was impossible to judge. Mr Douglas was well known in the Forres area as one of the all-time greats at storytelling. Certainly I had met keepers who claimed to have been killing the cats twenty years earlier, and

I had to agree wholeheartedly with Mr Douglas when he denied that the *Tomorrow's World* team had caught a Kellas.

Tomas's mounted cat was loaned to the Elgin Museum as one of its star attractions. He felt it was right that the animal should be placed on public display. The museum produced a superb poster picturing the head of the viciously snarling stuffed cat and the tale of the mystery cats faded out of the headlines, though not from public notice.

I still received reports of sightings of both the leopard-size cats and the smaller Kellas cats, but nothing dramatic happened until one night when I was driving through the forestry plantation from Forres to Dallas. Suddenly a black cat dashed out of the trees and leapt in front of the car, causing me to slam on my brakes. The animal turned and glared at me before flashing up the adjoining bank and leaping on to a large tree stump. There it crouched, its body twisted, glaring angrily at me, its bushy tail wrapped around the post. I opened my window and stared back, just a couple of feet from the snarling beast, and for one wonderful moment I was face to face with a living Kellas!

The cat was jet black, with the small white star on its chest and the sprinkling of long white guard hairs over its flanks and hind quarters. The head was small, held forward on an extended long slim neck, the ears flattened to the side of the head, the mouth open, the lips curled back revealing large sharp daggers of canines. One paw was raised in a threatening posture, claws extended as it dared me to challenge it on its own territory. But the most amazing sight were its eyes, huge glowing orange orbs filled with intelligence and hatred. I have never before seen such burning fury in an animal's gaze. I was excited, elated at seeing the creature for the first time in all its natural beauty, but I was totally unprepared for the shock of those huge living eyes.

For seconds we were both frozen in time, then the spell was broken. With one last vicious snarling growl, the Kellas cat leapt off the post and disappeared into the black depths of the tangled trees, leaving only a fleeting image of the short bushy tail, spangled with silvery stars in the moonlight, streaming behind it as it ran.

I sat behind the wheel of the car, the cold night air frosting my breath, stunned by the unexpectedness of the encounter. There was no way the study of the limp lank bodies with the dull cloudy eyes could have prepared me for the power and beauty of the living creature. There was an element of both fear and awe, a sensation of the supernatural in the meeting. I stared into the velvet darkness of the laced branches of the conifers and felt a sense of emptiness and loss, almost of bereavement, I could readily understand how the legends of the Highland Fairy Cat had begun.

The weeks passed and I had to find work. I took the job of reporter on a small rural paper in Keith, a town some thirty miles from Dallas. The job turned out to be writing almost the entire weekly paper, with the exception of the sports reports, the music review, the 'stars' and the adverts. I would leave Dallas at six-thirty in the morning and not return home some nights until eleven. It left no time for restoring the Dallas cottage, which was a major task, and so I looked for something to buy nearer Keith. Eventually I left the paper but settled into a house with four acres of land near the village of Drummuir where I could continue my cat research and write. Hundreds of sightings of the big cats, including five of my own in Scotland, were recorded and filed, while the deep freeze filled with dead Kellas specimens presented by the local gamekeepers. I extended my circle of friendly land-owners and keepers to cover a vast area of the north-east of Scotland.

One family near Nairn contacted me to say they had found a small black kitten in the wild, and hand reared and semi-tamed it. It had never become as friendly as a domestic cat but it purred on greeting them, slept on a rug in front of the fire, and ate domestic cat food despite proving itself to be an excellent hunter. As it reached adulthood it began to spend more and more time away from the house, until finally, it disappeared completely. Whether it had returned to the wild or met with a mishap the family had no way of knowing. Then one day, while visiting Elgin Museum, the children were suddenly confronted with what appeared to be their pet, stuffed and in a glass case, perched upon an enormous block of wood. The day ended in disaster with the children sobbing unconsolably at the cruel demise of their cherished pet.

I was able at least to comfort the family by assuring them that their pet had not ended up in the museum for their cat had been female whereas Tomas's cat was male. So whatever had happened to their cat, it had not been in Tomas's gun sights. The family was convinced the two cats were identical, and this posed an interesting question. Had the family really found and raised a Kellas cat? It was an intriguing thought.

The next person to contact me was a Richard Greenwell, the secretary of the International Society of Cryptozoology, who had read about the cats and was interested to hear how the research was progressing. Although based in the United States, he was shortly to be visiting Scotland and wanted to meet me. He also asked if I would be interested in addressing the society's next annual conference, which was being hosted by the Royal Museum of Scotland in Edinburgh. I accepted the invitation to speak and suggested that he should visit me when he came to Scotland.

I was thrilled by the approach, for the society had been founded by Dr Bernard Heuvelmans, whose book *On The Track Of Unknown Animals* I so much admired when I had read it some years earlier. The society had been formed to provide a forum for people involved in fringe scientific projects and to encourage establishment scientists to venture into researching the possibility of unknown or hidden animals existing throughout the world. One such creature was a big cat, the Onza.

Early Spanish chroniclers at the time of the Spanish conquest of Mexico in 1519 claimed that there were three wild big cats in the new continent – the tiger or jaguar, the lion or puma and the Onza, a puma-like cat which the Aztec called cuitlamiztli. The Onza was similar to the puma but of slimmer build with longer legs and with a much more aggressive nature than its shy cousin.

In the 1930s two hunting brothers, Dale and Clell Lee, heard tales of the existence of Onzas but it was not until 1938, when on a hunt in the San Ignacio District of Sinaloa, that they encountered a puma-like cat which showed extraordinary courage before being shot dead. On close examination, the animal exhibited marked differences from the puma: it was slimmer, longer-legged and with larger ears than the normal puma. The animal was measured and photographed and then forgotten until, in 1961, a book was written about the Onza by Robert Marshall. Then in 1985 Richard Greenwell, together with members of the ISC visited the area to investigate rumours of the existence of the third big cat species. A few months later Andres Rodriguez Murillo, a rancher in the area, shot a puma-like cat that appeared to be about to attack him. The animal resembled the legendary Onza.

The animal had been handed over to Greenwell's scientific team, and I looked forward to meeting the man whose research so closely paralleled my own work.

4

The Dufftown Specimen

The scientific staff of the Royal Museum of Scotland in Edinburgh have an open mind to the possibilities of new discoveries – even though the scientists there have a natural tendency to accept nothing at face value, I found them at least willing to consider new evidence and subject it to careful scrutiny. I was naturally cautious, but after talking to David Hepple, both a staff member at the Edinburgh museum and a director of the International Society of Cryptozoology, I agreed to take a complete frozen carcase of a Kellas for examination in their laboratory and a second mounted specimen to exhibit during my lecture.

I had now collected seven carcases including the Advie cat and Tomas' first cat. There were also the photographs of the missing Revack cat. If the scientists at the Edinburgh museum were willing to look, I certainly had the evidence to show them.

As luck would have it, three weeks before the Society's meeting, Colin Barclay, Tomas's gamekeeper, phoned to tell me he had received another Kellas specimen from a Dufftown gamekeeper, and it was waiting for me in the freezer. The freshly killed untouched carcase seemed the ideal specimen to take to the museum so I arranged to collect it the night before travelling to Edinburgh. That would give the specimen time to defrost before I handed it over. With the conference spread over two days, I would be in the city from Friday afternoon until Monday morning, time enough for the museum staff to examine the animal and remove any organs they required for further examination. I had no intention of giving them the carcase. It was coming home with me. My trust had not yet been altogether restored.

The ISC conference collected a fair amount of advance publicity. Richard Greenwell was giving a talk on his discovery of the Onza-like cat, others were to discuss king cheetahs and Australian marsupial felines, and of course my own subject had gained a good deal of press coverage over the years since the first report of the Revack cat. Two weeks before the meeting I started to receive phone calls demanding copies of my talk so that newspapers could complete their reviews before the actual event. I could not oblige them because I did not make notes, preferring to speak spontaneously on the subject I knew by heart. I tried to explain to callers that I had no intention of writing a speech and was treated with hostility and disbelief.

'Of course you use a prepared talk. Everyone does,' said one representative of a national newspaper.

'Well, I don't!' I said wearily.

'You must. You just don't want to let me have it,' the reporter growled. 'There are plenty of other speakers who will be only too glad to be reported.'

'Then you'd better contact them,' I snapped back and heard the phone slam down.

Richard Greenwell arrived with his young son the weekend before the conference and stayed for a couple of days. He was not at all what I had expected, and was certainly not like anyone the tiny rural town of Keith had encountered before. A small man with dark hair and a full dark beard, he was rather loud, dressed in a safari suit complete with bush hunter hat. Although English born and raised in the home counties, he had lived in the United States for a number of years and, like many immigrants, had become more American than

Americans. Despite the air he adopted of a great white hunter from Hollywood, I found him an amusing conversationist who easily dropped anecdotes of being lost in the jungles of South America or wading through the swamps of equatorial Africa in pursuit of the Congo dinosaur. He looked through my mass of evidence for the existence of the British Big Cat, and for the identity of the Kellas cats, and passed my work as acceptable to the society. I counted it an honour as most members of the society were also establishment zoologists and biologists. In fact the titles of Dr and Professor were so common among members that they kept to a rule against using titles in their publications.

We also discussed the native wildcat and the hybrid situation in Scotland. Richard told me that his local American museum had no wildcat skull in its collection. I knew that a number of wildcat carcases, either killed accidently or shot illegally, turned up in a number of gamekeeper's freezers, so I promised that I would bring one down to Edinburgh for him to take back to the States.

It is illegal to shoot wildcats as they are a protected species; snared cats, however, are deemed legal kills, and I knew Colin Barclay had a couple of snared wildcats in the freezer. I phoned him and he agreed to let Richard have one. It was a large male specimen which had been saved for mounting at a later date.

The first day of the conference was to be given over entirely to the search for and the history of the Loch Ness Monster, but the second day was to be almost exclusively devoted to mystery cats, with my talk starting the proceedings.

On Thursday I drove across to Kellas to collect the new Kellas cat and the genuine Scottish wildcat I had promised to take to Greenwell. Colin told me he hadn't had time to examine the new Kellas but it had been shot by a young keeper near Dufftown who had contacted him immediately and put the body in the freezer within an hour of its death. As the animal was wrapped up and deep frozen when he received it, Colin hadn't bothered to unpack it but had just dumped it in his own freezer for me to collect at a later date.

He first took out the wildcat, a magnificent specimen, in the upper size bracket, and then carefully unpacked the new Kellas specimen, dragging out the familar stiff elongated black dustbin bag parcel. The size was right, so was the shape, long and slim with rigidly folded elongated legs, but just as a precaution, I opened up the bag and shook the contents on to the floor, the white frosted carcase slithering out as a rock hard contorted parody of the living beast.

We both stared.

'My God!' I breathed.

Colin looked equally shocked. 'What the hell is it?'

The rigid body lay twisted before us, its long legs folded up and tucked into its body. It was a cat of Kellas size and build, long, lean and jet black, but there all resemblence ended. The cat had a large head with a pronounced Roman nose, big upright ears and an overshot upper jaw with huge protruding canine teeth that overhung the lower lip. Unlike the Kellas, the tail was long and slender, though muscular and whip-like. It looked altogether unlike a domestic cat. It was powerful, muscular and vicious-looking, a beautifully sleek and dangerous killing machine.

The creature's claws were extended in death, dog-like heavy blunt claws, not the razor sharp slender claws of the cat species. Was this a cub or young animal of the mystery big cat with its apparently non-retractile claws?

I dropped to my knees for a closer look at the carcase. Was it undeveloped? It was difficult to examine the animal properly because of its frozen state, but easily discernable below the tail were two fully developed testicles. The cat was an adult tom and it was too small to be a full grown big cat of leopard size.

I realised I was looking at a third mystery cat. The animal I had arranged to take to the Royal Museum of Scotland was not a Kellas. Fortunately I had other Kellas cats in the freezer but they had already had their internal organs removed. Still, there was no choice. I was catching the 6 a.m. train from Keith the next day and would be arriving in Edinburgh at lunchtime. I was to be met off the train by a member of the museum staff who was coming for the sole purpose of collecting a dead defrosting Kellas cat. There was no time to examine the Dufftown cat fully, so I decided to take it with me, together with another already gutted true Kellas specimen, the wildcat for Richard and of course the mounted specimen that I was displaying at the conference. Maybe the museum could throw some light on the origin of the Dufftown specimen.

As I stared at the cat I was struck by the shape of the head; it looked exactly like a rabbit with short ears. A rabbit-headed cat!

Next day, with three defrosting cats concealed in one suitcase and my clothes and slides for the lecture crammed in around the stuffed cat in another case, I was Edinburgh bound.

In my experience, British Rail in winter has a tendency to keep carriages just above freezing, but as this was summer the heating was on full blast. The train was packed with holidaymakers and my suitcases were jammed into the luggage rack, buckling under the weight of all the others shoved on top, including the luggage owned by the Dutch couple sitting opposite me. The Dutchman spent most of the journey wiping the sweat from his bald head and complaining bitterly in broken English.

'We have fresh farm eggs in our suitcase,' he wailed for the umteenth time to the guard. 'In this heat, they will all be cooked, no?'

The harrassed and equally cooked guard shook his head helplessly. 'I'm sorry, sir, there is nothing I can do, The thermostat has jammed. We can't turn the heating off.'

'But my eggs!' howled the Dutchman.

You think you've got problems, I mused as I wondered how the museum would respond to examining cooked cats. I watched anxiously for any sign of reddish liquid seeping out from under the luggage rack and it was with great relief that I disembarked at Edinburgh, dragging my weighty and suspiciously smelly suitcases on to the platform. Andrew Barker was waiting for me in the cool of the station.

A slim bearded man in his thiries met us in the car park. Philip Howard was the museum taxidermist who was going to examine the specimen I had brought with me. I explained my dilemma, that the expected Kellas cat I had been to collect had turned out not to be a Kellas nor anything else that I could recognize.

'I've brought it and a real Kellas for you to examine,' I said, 'but I'd like to show it to Andrew before you take it away.'

Philip Howard looked round uncertainly. I understood his feelings. The car park in Edinburgh station was not the most discreet spot in which to be examining dead cats, but I was determined that Andrew should see the Dufftown animal before it was skinned and dismembered on the laboratory slab.

Using the car boot lid and our own bodies to shield the sight from passing eyes, we unbagged the Dufftown cat and stretched the now limp carcase across the back of the car. As its now flexible limbs stretched out, its size became more apparent. If anything it was even bigger than the average Kellas specimens; it certainly dwarfed the wildcat.

'Well?'

We all stared down at the Dufftown cat. Now that it was relaxed it looked stranger than ever.

'It looks like a bloody rabbit,' Andrew said.

Philip Howard seemed unimpressed. 'It must be part Siamese,' he suggested.

I did not consider a crowded public car park was the ideal setting for a argument on the physical characteristics of a Siamese cat compared with the Roman-nose rabbit-headed feline that lay leaking before us.

'I'll have a good look at it in the Lab,' the taxidermist said, but I could see his eyes were on the Kellas.

'Thanks,' I said. 'But I've not got a photographic record of this new cat, so could you please take some shots of it before you start cutting it up?'

The taxidermist nodded. 'Now, I must get these back to the museum. We are going to be pushed for time if you want me to clean the other two skulls as well as the Kellas.' I had to let him go and just hoped he would keep his promise.

After a meal in the museum restaurant I was begining to feel nervous at the thought of standing up before all those critical academics. Noticing swing doors marked 'Lecture Hall, No Admittance', I signalled to Andrew that I was sneaking off into forbidden territory.

I walked quietly up on to the platform and stared at the daunting rows of raised seats before me. I imagined the sensation of all those staring and possibly unfriendly eyes. Mentally I put faces in the empty spaces and bottoms on seats, and then I felt better. I knew when my turn came on Sunday morning I could ignore the audience, whatever it was like, I'd already seen them and faced them.

A museum security man appeared, glowering through the swing doors.

'I'm afraid this area is not open to the public,' he growled.

I nodded. 'I know,' I said, smiling at him as I stepped off the platform. 'I'm speaking here on Sunday and just wanted to get the feel of the place. I'm going now.'

He watched me suspiciously as I rejoined Andrew and we left the room.

It was strange but I was no longer insecure or nervous. I could ignore the hostility I knew would be there while I was putting forward the case for the existence of the big cat and shrug off the derision I had constantly faced from the academic world. I was ready for them.

The next stop was the local radio station. Richard, myself and the Canadian oceanographer Paul LeBlond, one of the Nessie speakers, were booked to appear on the *Jimmy MacGregor Show*. Talks by the other two were going out before the conference but my recorded interview was not being used until after the weekend, the slight complication being that I would have to speak as if everything were over and say what a great success the meeting had been.

Richard and Paul recorded their interviews first, while Andrew and I sat on the sidelines, hearing just one half of the conversation. Like the Inverness television studio, Edinburgh was radio-linked to Glasgow where Jimmy McGregor was located, so the interview took place in an empty room, the questions coming through the headphones that only the person being interviewed wore. When it was my turn, Jimmy's chirpy voice rang in my ears as he asked about the Kellas cats. He told me he'd wanted to look me up when he had been doing a television programme on the Speyside Walk but had been short of time. He had seen one of my stuffed black cats when he was at Tomintoul.

As it was a recorded interview I was able to ask questions myself, knowing that all surplus conversation could be wiped off the tape. I said I didn't know of a Kellas specimen at Tomintoul.

'A magnificent beast,' Jimmy said cheerfully.

'What specimen?' I demanded suddenly, turning the tables on the interviewer. 'What cat did you see?'

'One of your black Morayshire mystery cats,' he said in some surprise.

'What did it look like?'

'A big black cat, the size of a Scottish wildcat. Had white hairs in its coat.'

'But how was it mounted?'

'Er, on a piece of wood, I think.'

'Where was its front paw?'

'Its paw?'

'Yes, was it up or down?'

'It was up and the cat was crouched on a very large sort of tree stump.'

I relaxed. It had to be Tomas's cat. The Elgin Museum must have loaned it out. It wasn't a specimen I didn't know about. I went back to answering his questions about the conference.

Saturday was the day of the Loch Ness monsters and a number of well-known figures took their places on the platform, some of whom gave interesting information while others, I felt, were really just milking the subject.

Dr Robert H. Rines was one man with whom I had a lot of sympathy. He threw back criticism to the 'debunkers and writers of books' who had attempted to discredit the famous underwater photographs of the head and flipper of 'Nessie' which he had been involved in taking in the 1970's. Whether or not he really had photographed the monster I didn't know, but he believed he had, and I recognized his feelings of frustration as those I had suffered over my own big cat photos.

A highlight of the day was the last speaker, Tim Dinsdale, an aeronautical engineer who, while on holiday in Scotland in the 1960s, had filmed something suspicious on the loch and from then on had devoted his life to proving that an unknown creature lived in its peaty waters. For thirty years he had studied, photographed and written on the subject. He was rewarded with Honorary Membership of the Society, and I was lucky enough to meet him afterwards. A quiet, unassuming man who had become a legend in the world of cryptozoology, sadly he died just a few months later, his self-appointed task – to prove the existence of an unknown creature in the Scottish loch – still uncompleted.

On Sunday morning I was relaxed and ready to kick the day's proceedings into start. I decided to have a bit of fun. The previous day's lectures had all been on the serious side, only Dr Rines adding a touch of humour, and as I couldn't match the Latin terminology or the university qualifications, I would aim for entertainment value. Before starting, I had a quiet word with the man in the projection room.

'When I give the signal,' I told him, 'would you please play this recording.'

I then concealed the Kellas specimen in its obligatory black dustbin bag under the stage and arranged for Richard's son to pass it to me at another signal. Now I was ready for the audience, which, incidentally, had shrunk from the previous day's numbers. It seemed that mystery cats had less appeal than loch monsters.

I began by rattling on about the history of the search for the big cats and explained the slides of indistinct giant cats on Welsh hillsides and half eaten sheep. Then I said sweetly –

'If one of the cats themselves could be here, I'm sure they'd like to have the last word on the subject.' I signalled to the projection box and the auditorium was suddenly filled with the terrifying echoing scream of the big cat recorded on the Welsh hillside. The effect was electrifying. It certainly woke any would-be sleepers with a start.

I launched into a quick background description of the Kellas cats, their discovery and description, emphasising the normal retractable claws, small size and inability to kill anything as large as a sheep. Then I signalled to Richard's son, who passed the black bag up to me.

'One last thing, I would like to introduce you all to a friend who hasn't paid his entrance fee,' I whipped off the cover and held the stuffed Kellas on high.

I was given a solid round of applause and flashing camera lights. I had done it.

The following morning I collected my specimens from the museum before setting off to catch the 11.55 train home. The stuffed Kellas was once more crammed into my suitcase, with my clothing carefully packed around it. At 11.30, while I was gulping back a cup of coffee and saying my goodbyes, I packed the two cat carcases into the second suitcase and shoved a box containing the stripped skulls into my handbag. I was just leaving when a telephone call came through to the museum for me. BBC Television wanted to film the Kellas cat. I said I was sorry but there was less than half an hour before my train left and I was just on my way to the station.

'That's all right,' said a soothing voice, 'we'll meet you on the platform.'

'But the cat is packed in my suitcase,' I wailed.

'See you in a few minutes,' said the voice calmly, ignoring my wail.

The phone went dead. I gathered my belongings and with

Andrew leapt into a waiting taxi. We arrived at the station five minutes before the train was due to leave.

A BBC camera crew was assembled on the platform, accompanied by an unruffled, tall and immaculately dressed presenter with a toothpaste smile.

'Now, if you will just unpack the cat, we'll film you,' he said.

Puffing, sweating, and very ruffled, I gasped – 'But the train . . . it's due!'

'We've plenty of time,' soothed the flashing smile confidently. 'Now, if you'll just show us the cat.'

'Here on the platform?' I looked around me at the sea of curious faces that always gather at the sight of blood or a television camera. The presenter nodded calmly.

I was browbeaten by the contained assurance. Who was I to dare question such a professional? I bent down to undo the case containing the mounted Kellas as the camera whirred, then I remembered my padding of underwear.

I turned to the cameraman. 'I'm sorry, you'll have to stop running until I've sorted out my clothing,' I snapped coldly, hastily removing a bra strap that had hooked itself around the cat's teeth. I glanced up at the station clock. It was six minutes to twelve.

I hauled the cat out of the bag and waved it triumphantly in the air. 'You've got just one minute,' I said.

'Oh, we've plenty of time.'

The cameraman started filming and the presenter began his interview in a bright voice.

'Di, I believe you had some rather exciting news for. . . .'

With a shrill screech the train thundered into the station and I could see the presenter's lips moving without hearing a word he said. I shrugged, grabbed my bag, suitcases and stuffed cat and began to run down the platform through the watching crowds, Andrew ahead of me on his longer legs, both of us pursued by the cameraman and the soundman, the two attached to each other by a cable that looked like a giant umbilical cord.

Andrew pulled open a door and slung my suitcases inside. I followed, clutching the stuffed cat. It wasn't a moment too soon. The train started to move as I yelled my goodbyes and spotted the TV presenter, looking just very slightly ruffled, racing after us. As the train gathered speed I noticed that the cameraman was still filming. I hung the cat out of the train window to wave a stiffened paw. Then we were out of the station and the figures on the platform were gone. I gathered up my cases and turned to enter the carriage, still clutching the aggressive stuffed cat.

I was confronted by rows of shocked and curious faces. The other passengers had watched the whole fiasco through the windows. Self-consciously I undid my suitcase and pushed the cat back into its padding and reclosed the case. After placing the cases on the rack, I found a seat and opened my bag to fish out something to read. There was the box containing the Kellas and the Dufftown cat skulls. I was curious to see the shape of the skull of the Roman-nosed feline; did it look any different to that of a normal cat? After all, as I had often been told, a cat is a cat is a cat!

I put my bag on my lap and rummaged through, shoving things into corners to make space in which to open the lid of the box. Carefully I ripped off the sealing tape and eased up the lid. The skulls were packed in polystyrene chips which blew up into my face as someone behind opened the sliding door.

Once the polystyrene storm had settled, I peered down at the two skulls nestling side by side in their cardboard coffer. The Kellas skull was smooth, domed, gleaming polished white ivory, exactly like all the others, and very similar to both domestic and wildcat skulls. The differences between the small cat species skulls were subtle, a slight variation of shape and brain capacity, nothing startling, nothing outstanding. The other skull was longer and heavier than the Kellas, but the domed brain case was about half the size of the other one, and instead of the smooth ivory gleam of polished bone, the second skull was creamy yellow, textured and pitted like a piece of plastic cheese. The skull inside that strange Roman-nosed rabbit-headed cat was even weirder than the cat's outside appearance.

Whatever I was looking at, it certainly wasn't a cat like a cat!

Why hadn't Philip Howard mentioned the differences when he gave me back the skull? Why hadn't I looked at it while I was still at the museum? Surely there could not be a third mystery cat?

I tried to recall the outward appearance of the Dufftown animal but my glimpses of it had been so fleeting, I could only remember the first shock of it not being a Kellas, and then its strange rabbit-like appearance, the long flat skull, the odd bulging nose, the almost slanting eyes and the large upright thinly-furred ears.

I closed the box, shutting away the skulls and the puzzle and sat staring out of the window, watching the Scottish countryside slip by, hills becoming mountains, vast stretches of heather and bracken-covered moors, the long black streaks of forestry plantations, with small farms and lonely crofts scattered about bleak but beautiful stoney valleys. So much space, so little human habitation. Even less than there used to be, as was shown by the tiny piles of tumbled stone walls and ruined cottages that littered the moorlands, reminders of generations of farmers and shepherds finally driven from their land by financial desperation, politics or the harshness of the climate.

But if the humans no longer farmed or hunted over the Highland hills, what else prowled the wild places, stalking the plentiful game, sheltering from the inclement climate in the dark secure warmth of the closely growing conifers?

5

A Live Kellas Trapped

Breakfast the following morning consisted of coffee, toast and puzzlement. If the Dufftown skull had looked strange in the fleeting glimpses I had managed on the train, more detailed examination did nothing to change my impression. The skull was altogether different from the domestic, the wildcat and the Kellas skulls lined up for comparism. In contrast to the ivory white polished bone of the other three skulls, the Dufftown animal had a fibrous gnarled, almost woven texture. It was a creamy-honey in colour, with a rather waxy feel, and the shape unlike any of the others. Nothing about it matched any of the other skulls.

The Dufftown skull was large, longer than even the wildcat's, but the cranial capacity was about half the size of the other cats'. A big head with a small brain. The structure of the skull, especially the jaw, was heavy, giving the impression of tremendous power, the jaw long, broad and solid. The eardrums were larger than those of the other cats, the upper jaw projecting over the lower, the nasal passage very broad, with grooves on either side where the lower canines fitted snugly against the cheek when the mouth was closed. The teeth were the most startling feature. The Dufftown canines were extremely long, like those of a prehistoric false sabre-tooth, and the upper jaw, although longer than the other

71

cats', had bony ridges where four of the upper premolars should have been. The Dufftown cat hadn't lost its four missing teeth; they had never been there. The incisors were also strange. Instead of the upper and lower tiny front teeth abutting on to each other in a neat straight line, the Dufftown's incisors were pointed, so that when the jaw was closed the teeth interlocked, giving a shark-like bite that would rip off the prey's flesh in large chunks. When the mouth was shut, there were indentations in both upper and lower jaws that accommodated the teeth like a smoothly fitting jigsaw. The skull did not appear to be mutated, rather it seemed to have evolved into a shape to accommodate the perfect killing machine – a sort of feline shark, a hunter with a highly developed sense of smell and acute hearing, a tremendously powerful bite but with limited intelligence. A primitive but lethal hunter.

I deeply regretted that I had not taken the opportunity to examine the body properly before the museum stripped it. I had asked Philip Howard to photograph the animal before skinning it, and he had taken just three shots. One of the whole animal showed clearly the long lean body, slim graceful legs, smooth coat and whip-like slender tail. A creature built for speed. Two other photographs showed only the head: one was indistinct, attempting to show the bulbous Roman nose; the other, a profile, clearly illustrating the rabbit shape with its hooked sabre teeth, overshot upper jaw, dog-like nose and long flat skull with its huge naked upright ears.

I phoned Philip and asked his opinion of the animal. Surely the scientists could not deny that this creature was different.

They could, and did.

'Undoubtedly a domestic cat,' I was informed airily.

'But what about the shape of the head?' I asked.

'Probably a cross with a Siamese. They have that sort of head.'

Years before I had bred Siamese cats; their heads were nothing like the Dufftown specimen. I tried a different tack, the missing teeth.

'Oh, cats often lose teeth, especially old ones.'

'But these aren't lost, they've never been there.'

'They will have been. The sockets have just got filled in with a boney residue. It often happens.'

I tried one more point. 'The actual bone texture is different, sort of fibrous.'

'Like the missing teeth. It's because this was an old animal. Sorry, it's just a domestic feral, or maybe a hybrid, nothing unusual.'

I gave up.

Whatever the Dufftown was, hybrid or species, it was nothing like a Siamese cat, which has a small pointed face and delicate bone structure. It was clear to me that once again the scientists were dismissing something strange without examining it properly. I was quite willing to believe the new cat was an escaped exotic, or perhaps even a hybrid between an exotic and a domestic or wildcat, or even a combination of all three, but I could not accept the strange creature as no more than an old domestic cat or a domestic wildcat hybrid, with or without Siamese blood.

I decided to contact Charles Thomas. He was intrigued and agreed to take the skull to Frank Turk for examination. In some trepidation I posted the Dufftown skull, praying that the GPO wouldn't lose it. The thought of the strange skull gathering dust on a Post Office shelf for years was not a happy one.

Fortunately the parcel arrived safely and Dr Turk was able to study the skull in detail. He found no evidence of the missing teeth ever having existed. It seemed that Philip Howard was mistaken. It was not just an old animal that had lost its teeth, but knowing what it wasn't took us no nearer to finding out what it was. I compared the measurements with records of other skulls in the British Museum's collection. One skull appeared to have a similar small cranial capacity combined with overall large dimensions. The animal was listed as a hybrid domestic wildcat from Hungary. It was a long shot but I wondered if the Hungarian skull had missing teeth in the upper jaw and interlocking front incisors.

With some misgivings I decided to ring Daphne Hills, who I felt had at least tried to be fair, and ask her for information about the Hungarian skull. She was not over-helpful. If I wanted a photograph of the skull, it would take some weeks for their photographer to arrange it and I would have to pay for the privilege.

Andrew Barker lived in London and I knew he would be willing to pop across to the museum to take a couple of snaps of the Hungarian skull for me, so that I could compare it with the Dufftown animal. If they seemed similar, that would be the time to arrange for expensive professional photographs to be taken.

I said cheerfully that I understood how busy they were and, rather than take up their photographer's time, I could arrange for someone to call in to take a couple of shots.

I was told that only their photographer could take the photographs. I asked Daphne Hills if the museum had agreed to pay my expenses, which amounted to a couple of thousand pounds, for providing the Advie carcase. She had the grace to sound contrite and said she'd see what she could arrange.

Sometime later I received a letter, dated 8th September 1987, in which she said she had consulted her head of section, Mr I. R. Bishop, and he had confirmed that any photographs of the Hungarian skull would have to be taken by the museum's photographic unit. If I gave written assurance that the pictures would not be published, the museum would arrange for some prints to be sent to me at no charge. This was to be regarded as a reciprocal arrangement for the presentation of the cat from Advie. The letter finished with the comment that internal requisitions are not given the same priority as commercial work, so there could be some delay. Daphne Hills offered to complete the appropriate forms as soon as she heard from me.

I was angry. The museum had already made money out of my work by selling it to the BBC. To put it simply, they could stuff their photographs! As far as I am concerned the British Museum of Natural History is still in my debt.

I never did find out if the Hungarian skull bore any resemblence to the Dufftown cat, but rumours were abounding that the Kellas type of cat could be found across Europe. It seemed that the Scottish Kellas cats and Satunin's demon cats were not alone; there were numerous reports of fierce black wildcats which made it all the more difficult to understand the lack of interest shown in official scientific circles.

At this time I was corresponding with Dr Bernard Heuvelmans in Paris, a man who had given his entire life and career to investigating the existence of unclassified creatures throughout the world. He was a brilliant academic, the author of numerous books on the subject including the bible of the science of cryptozoology, *On the Track of Unknown Animals*, and founder of the International Society of Cryptozoology. I was heartened by both his support and the knowledge that he had frequently battled with establishment scientists who dismissed evidence and refused to face facts. I could not send the skull out of the country for fear it would get damaged, or mislaid, and I could not afford to have copies made, so I decided to wait until the International Society held their next annual meeting in Britain and then take the skull to show Dr Heuvelmans personally while he was attending the conference.

Richard Greenwell was in London and I agreed to travel down from Scotland to meet him and show him both the Dufftown skull and a second unidentified skull found on Dartmoor of a lion-size cat that I suspected belonged to the big mystery cat I had investigated on Exmoor. I met him in his hotel and laid the lion-size skull in front of him. He was fascinated by its huge canines and powerful structure. Then I produced the smaller but equally powerful Dufftown skull. Richard examined it closely.

'I don't know what it is,' he admitted. 'I've never seen anything like it.'

He agreed to take tiny shavings of bone from both skulls back to America and there try to persuade the scientific team working on the Onza specimens, to attempt a genetic identification of the mystery British skulls.

In the following March news filtered through of an exciting event in the Kellas investigation. Scottish newspapers reported the capture of a fierce wild black cat. Mr Tony Sill of Redcastle in Ross-shire had become fed up with the antics of an unknown predator that had carried off eighteen of his Aylesbury ducks, leaving him just two. The forestry worker decided enough was enough and built a trap to capture the animal, thinking it must be a well-fed fox. One Sunday morning he found the trap sprung and not a fox snarling at him in fury but a huge black cat – a black cat the size of a small dog with a short bushy tail, with a white spot on its chest and long white guard hairs scattered throughout its jet black coat.

A living Kellas?

The photographs revealed a large but proportionally normal-looking black cat with a short clubbed tail, lean long body and long slender legs. A typical Kellas shape. In the black and white press pictures the cat appeared to have a large white flash down the face and one front leg, but on closer examination I was fairly sure that the marks were not markings in the coat, but raw skinned patches where the unfortunate animal had battered itself in a frenzy to escape from the trap.

I had no proof but I was sure the Ross-shire cat, which had been taken to the Highland Wildlife Park, was a true Kellas, the first to be captured and kept alive if one disregarded the questionable much smaller cat trapped by the *Tomorrow's World* programme. I decided to say nothing but to monitor the situation quietly. It was frustrating to suspect the first living Kellas specimen was in captivity and I did not have access to it.

A change of staff at the Royal Museum of Scotland produced a new curator of mammals and birds. The arrival of Dr Andrew Kitchener, a young man with a reputation of talent combined with youthful energy and enthusiasm, was good for the museum's image and also proved good for the Kellas cat research. Dr Kitchener took a keen interest in the mystery black cats, and although he believed them to be the result of hybridization between the Scottish wildcat and domestic ferals, he was also convinced they were an important and interesting discovery. Unlike the Natural History Museum in London, which had dismissed them as unimportant, Dr Kitchener thought that their origins were worth a serious scientific study. He suspected the Kellas cats had been around for a long time, possibly a hundred years or more, a genetic combination that had become firmly established within the feline population. He did not treat me as a minor irritation but took the time and trouble to explain his views and suggested that I should let him see all my material so that he could set up a full scientific study of the animals.

It was exactly what I had wanted, and after a few minor disagreements about the ownership of the material I was providing, I agreed to give him access to all my specimens. I was unwilling to relinquish ownership as I knew from bitter experience I could then be dismissed and lose any control of the results. If I was prepared to trust Andrew Kitchener personally, I no longer had any faith in establishment science. He was just one man, one voice; if he moved on, a new less enlightened man could take over the Kellas research at the museum.

An example of the type of disagreement that could occur arose during discussions about the method of preparing the skins of the Kellas carcases. I wanted the animals mounted to look as they had in life and then circulated around the countryside to show gamekeepers and landowners just what we were interested in. Telling them that we wanted news of large black cat sightings was one thing, showing the actual animals was much more likely to arouse their interest. Dr Kitchener wanted the animals to remain as study skins, soft shapeless stuffed sausages that remained stored in boxes until required by other scientists. Finally we settled on a compromise: some of the specimens would be mounted and some kept as study skins.

I kept in contact with all the gamekeepers involved in the cat research. Ronnie Douglas, who had trapped the first cat on the Revack Estate, had given up gamekeeping to become an officer of the SSPCA (the Scottish Society for Prevention of Cruelty to Animals) in Inverness. Unfortunately he had not been there when the Ross-shire cat had been captured, but I intended to hear about any future such captures first hand. I asked him to let me know if any more Kellas-type cats were found in his area. He agreed cheerfully and then told me he had recently bumped into the long missing taxidermist, Ronnie Buchan, to whom he'd sent the Revack cat. The taxidermist was working now as a gillie near Archiestown and still had the Revack cat in his freezer. With rough directions on how to find him, I set off once more on a Revack cat hunt. At his home I was told he was working on the Spey River bank, and it was there that I stood at last facing the man I had once been so desperate to meet. He was standing in the river, the water almost to the top of his waders.

'Mr Buchan?' I shouted. He looked up in surprise.

'Er, yes.'

'I've been looking for you for seven years,' I announced. He looked alarmed. 'I'm Di Francis!'

He acknowledged me with a wave and splashed towards me. 'You want the cat?' he said. 'I've got it somewhere in the freezer.'

Better late than never.

Unfortunately my triumph was shortlived. He had part of the cat, rather than the cat, in his freezer. The body and the skull were gone, only the rolled up skin remained, and when unravelled, even that was found to be missing the tail.

Still, at least I could look at the mask-like head and agree with Ronnie Douglas that whatever the Revack cat had been it had been big.

Sometime afterwards I received a phone call from Colin Barclay, the gamekeeper at Kellas, who gave me some news that, when relayed to Andrew Kitchener, caused a ripple of excitement at the Edinburgh museum. A female Kellas had been shot that morning, but it was a Kellas with a difference. It was heavily pregnant and the injury to the animal's side revealed the head of an unborn striped wildcat kitten. The female had died instantly and there had been no way in which to save the unborn kittens. Colin had placed the body immediately in the freezer as he thought it would interest me.

Interest me? That was the understatement of the year! It appeared to be the first real evidence that the black cats were definitely breeding with Scottish wildcats. I was saddened by the death of her innocent young kits which had been blasted from their mother's womb, but it was the law of the countryside. The cat had made the fatal mistake of counting on the estate's pheasant pens as a source of food, and it was a mistake she paid dearly for making. At the same time her death and that of her kits could provide a mass of genetic material for the scientists to use in the laboratory to help solve the mystery of the cat's origins.

'If the gamekeeper is right, then this new specimen is very important,' Andrew Kitchener said to me. 'Make sure it goes straight into the freezer.'

It was already in one, I assured him, together with the other five Kellases and the Dufftown cat. With so many black cat bodies safely preserved, waiting collection by the museum, and a live Kellas lurking, sulking and hidden in the Highland Wildlife Park, it seemed only a matter of time before the Kellas cats would reveal their true identity.

Unfortunately not everyone was willing to wait for the official investigation to be completed. An article appeared in the *Mail on Sunday*, written by reporter Peter Steele, describing the first Kellas specimen as 'a ferocious beast nearly four ft long with fangs, claws and legs of a panther. And the bushy 20 inch tall wildcat may have brought fear from the Scottish Highlands to Exmoor in Devon.'

If the description of the animal was not muddled enough, he ended his article with the absurd theory that 'because it is now illegal to keep panthers or pumas without a licence, some may have been released into the wild and mated with large domestic cats.'

A hybrid between a panther and a domestic cat? What rubbish! The only way a domestic cat and a panther could meet in the wild and become linked is for the domestic cat to end up as dinner inside the larger cat! Scarcely a senario for happy families.

It was like the obviously slim-legged captive Ross-shire cat being described as having 'legs the thickness of a man's arm' in March 1988, or the *Tomorrow's World* programme suggesting a cat the size of a large domestic could be responsible for killing and eating full grown sheep.

Soon after the shooting of this female cat Andrew Kitchener phoned me with some exciting news. As a member of the committee of the Royal Zoological Gardens in Edinburgh he was also involved with the management of the Highland Wildlife Park that now held the two captive mystery black cats, one of which I was sure was a Kellas.

'I don't know if you are interested,' he said casually. 'But I believe the wildlife park is looking for a new home for the *Tomorrow's World* cat and the Ross-shire black cat. If you were to contact them and offer a home, I think you'd have a good chance of getting them.'

I was stunned. A chance not just to see the Ross-shire cat but actually to own it? I had long dreamt of studying a living Kellas but as the years passed so the dream had faded.

Could that fading dream now suddenly come true?

6

Time Running Out

I was fortunate to be living where I could offer a home to the two cats. My cottage with four acres of land was in a rural situation on the outskirts of a small hamlet of eight dwellings in a wooded valley, surrounded by the heather-covered foothills of the Grampian mountains. I was not isolated, but I already owned a number of animals, including a couple of Clydesdale horses and a small flock of Hebridean sheep, so I hoped the addition of a cat pen in the middle of the goats, sheep, geese, hens and horses would go unnoticed.

Although I found it hard to believe the cats would be given to me, Andrew was on the zoo committee and he seemed pretty certain of his facts. I phoned the Highland Wildlife Park. An answering machine blandly thanked me for my call. It was a machine I became well aquainted with over the following three weeks. The park, of course, was closed to the public in the winter months and I supposed that no one bothered to check the calls – or perhaps the machine had gone wrong and no one had noticed the fault. It seemed to be a repetition of the Revack cat situation. Then one day the dull drawl of the recorded message was replaced by a cheerful human voice. I was so accustomed to the taped message that I almost automatically replaced the receiver.

I said I had heard from Andrew Kitchener that they were

looking for new homes for the black cats and asked if I could be considered as their new guardians? I expected a horrified no. Surely the cats were an immense public draw. They had received enormous publicity as the Morayshire mystery cats and a good number of people must have gone to the park especially to see them as a result of the media coverage. 'We got your messages,' the cheerful voice said. 'Hasn't Jeremy been back to you?'

I assured the voice that no, neither Jeremy nor anyone else had returned my frantic calls.

'Sorry about that. We've been a bit busy here. I know he intended to contact you.'

'Are you really looking for a home for the cats?' I asked.

'I think so,' the voice replied. 'You'll have to talk to Jeremy. He's the manager here now. I know there have been discussions about rehousing them because the park is being restructured.'

I was given a time to phone Jeremy Usher Smith, the new park manager, but every time I called I was told I had just missed him, or that he was expected but hadn't yet arrived. Then, after another week of frustration, Mr Usher Smith himself phoned me.

Yes, he confirmed, they were wanting to find a new home for the two black cats, and yes, Andrew Kitchener had indeed proposed that they might be placed with me. He could see no difficulties at all provided that I was willing to house them adequately. If I put my offer formally in writing it would be put officially to the committee at the next meeting.

I was overjoyed. They still hadn't agreed that I could have the cats but, with Andrew's support, it seemed I had a good chance of acquiring them. The only living captive Kellases might soon be mine. That very day I wrote the letter offering to house the cats.

Eagerly I watched the post for their answer. And I watched, and watched in vain. Weeks, then months, passed with neither agreement nor refusal. Christmas came and went, the year 1990 became '91, and I had given up. Either they were not getting rid of the cats after all or else I was not considered suitable.

Towards the end of January Andrew Kitchener phoned me to ask how the cats were doing.

'The cats?'

'Yes. How are the black cats settling into their new home?'

'I haven't the faintest idea,' I said, rather acidly, 'I haven't got them.'

'But I thought you were having them?'

'I offered,' I said, 'but I didn't even receive the courtesy of a reply.'

Andrew was confused. 'I know you offered,' he said, 'I was at the meeting when your offer was put before the Board – and it was accepted. It was agreed you should have the cats as a gift. I thought you would have them safely settled in by now.'

'But they've never been in touch. They didn't even acknowledge my letter.'

'Well, they got it, and they agreed you could have the cats last year. I thought I'd give them time to settle in before asking how they were getting on.'

'Well, whoever's got them, it isn't me, I'm afraid.'

'Look, don't worry, they are coming to you. I'll give Jeremy a ring and get it sorted out. They'll be in touch.'

I put down the phone and gave a wild whoop to the startled slumbering cats and dogs scattered around the room.

The cats were going to be mine! I was going to own the first live Kellas cat! I danced round the room watched by horrified canine and domestic feline eyes. Had I gone totally mad? They had always suspected that their human charge was a little odd, now they must have been wondering what the SSPCA accommodation was like.

The intoxication of the moment vanished as the practicalities of the situation took over. Because I hadn't known I was to have the cats, no enclosure had been prepared for them. When I had offered to house them, I had some money to hand and workmen engaged on modernising the house, so it would have been a simple matter to divert the men for a few days and get them to build suitable accommodation. Now the workmen were gone and the coffers were empty.

Joy turned to panic, a panic that had not dispersed when some days later I received a phone call from Jeremy Usher Smith.

'Sorry you weren't informed that your offer to house the cats had been accepted. When would you like to collect them?'

I said that I needed time to prepare for them. If I could look at the cats' enclosure in the park it would give me some idea of what was required. It was agreed. I would go across to see them and discuss the building plan.

The following week I was on my way to Kincraig with my friend Lynn, using her four-wheel drive to go through the mountains. I knew to my cost how quickly the early spring sunshine could change in Scotland to Arctic conditions, with deep snow and temperatures below zero.

I was going to see the captive Kellas at last! But things in my life seldom go according to carefully laid plans.

It was a cold mid-February day, the sky was a deep blue, the snow-capped mountains glinting with a golden sheen as the sun's rays touched the lower white crusted slopes, their heads lost in a distant blue haze that hinted of summer to come. The stark bare branches of the trees were trimmed with the first buds and the grass showed green in the valleys where cattle grazed contentedly. The lochs still carried a thick coating of pearly ice but there was a feeling of growth and awakening in the crisp air. As we drove through the ski resort of Aviemore, the main street was strangely quiet, a holiday town in waiting. The winter sports enthusiasts had departed with the thinning icy snow and there was a long time yet before the drift of summer visitors. We followed the tourist trail to the Highland Wildlife Park and drove into the deserted car park. I could hardly contain my excitment. Was I right? Was the Ross-shire cat really a Kellas? Soon I would know.

As it was out of season the route from the car park was

blocked by a barrier, so we located a track that wound its way through the deer enclosures to arrive at a group of buildings that housed the administrative offices.

Jeremy Usher Smith greeted me earnestly, a slim and bearded man who looked typical of so many of those involved with wildlife projects.

'I'll take you up to the black cat enclosure,' he said.

'I can't wait to see them,' I said.

He paused. 'Oh, I doubt that you'll see them. They spend the daytime in their sleeping accommodation, and if they do venture out, anyone strange approaching within half a mile of them will send them straight back into cover. I'm afraid your chances of seeing them are virtually nil.'

He was right. Lynn and I saw the wolves, including the Alpha female, the pack leader, and were introduced to the lynxes, magnificent big cats with friendly golden eyes, prowling the perimeter of their enclosure with a complete disregard of onlookers and a terrible stench of tom-cat. We even saw the genuine Scottish wildcat, sprawled among the branches of a small tree in its pen. But the objects of my interest, the two mystery black cats, were absent from their enclosure, presumably tucked cosily up together in the small wooden tree house.

I willed them at least to stick their heads out of their tiny high rise apartment to see what the commotion was about but there was no sign of life, just an empty pen and silence. The Morayshire mystery cats intended to remain a mystery.

The enclosure was smaller than I had expected, a wire and wood construction with the box-like sleeping accommodation set high in the tree and another den of stone and earth dug into the floor.

'They've a choice of sleeping quarters but they never seem to use the ground house,' we were told.

There was little point in standing and staring at a deserted enclosure. After making a mental note of the wire mesh fencing used, I accepted an offer for us to be shown round the new visitors' centre, where we were introduced to a pair of delightful polecats which lived in the office like household cats. Their duties were to assist in the teaching of school parties. The floor was criss-crossed with empty pipe through which the incorrigable pair raced and tumbled in a whirlwind of play before clambering up on to any available lap to collapse in soft fawn furry heaps and indulge in an orgy of tickles and petting. Although I had never considered polecats to be ideal pets, the pair completely won me over, their pungent scent being the only drawback to their winning the pet of the year award.

I agreed to start building the cat's enclosure as soon as possible but said that I thought there was little chance of it being ready before August. With that, Lynn and I took our leave and drove home through the mountains. I was disappointed. I still didn't know for certain if the Ross-shire cat was a Kellas, but at least I was reassured that the expected enclosure would not be too difficult to construct and did not have to be of stronger materials than wire and wood.

Over the next few weeks I designed the accommodation that would be most suitable for the welfare and comfort of the animals, but I couldn't afford to pay for it to be built. The greatest stumbling block was the required type of wire mesh. This had to be a very strong gauge spot welded mesh, not the chain link sort that was most widely available. The chain link type consists of long strands of wire interlocked to make a diamond-shape mesh and is the type used for stock fencing and normal security purposes. These twisted strands are flexible and the links can slip apart with pressure, making them unsuitable for a cat that would attempt to climb the mesh. After inserting its claws into the crossover joints, the wire could then close over claws and paws, trapping the unfortunate animal and crushing its feet or tearing off toes or claws. On the other hand the spot-welded mesh has every joint welded rigid, making it completely safe for a climbing animal. It is also very expensive and therefore is restricted in supply. So restricted that I couldn't find a firm in Scotland that manufactured the stuff.

1   Tomas Christie's stuffed Kellas cat on the back seat of the author's car.

2   A female Scottish wildcat photographed at the Highland Wildlife Park by Rod Williams.

3   The BBC 'Tomorrow's World' cat, a female, the first live Kellas cat to be caught.

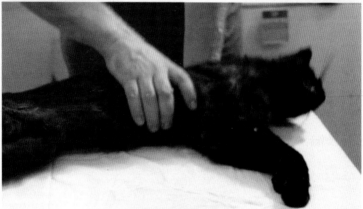

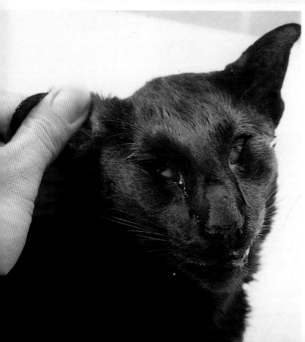

4   The Revack cat snared
by Ronnie Douglas and
photographed by the
Highland vet George
Rafferty.

5   The Advie cat being
photographed by Andrew
Barker before it is taken to
the Natural History
Museum in London.

6   The Dufftown cat with
its Roman nose
photographed in Philip
Howard's laboratory.

7 (right) The male Kellas caught in Ross-shire and kept in the Highland Wildlife Park.

8 (below) Tomas Christie's male Kellas in typical attacking pose.

9 (below) The breeding pen at the author's home where she watched her Kellas family develop.

10 The author's home in north-east Scotland where she built her Kellas cat pen.

11 Approaching the pen calls forth the Kellas attack.

12 Di Francis at home with her Clydesdale mare and its foal.

The weeks passed while I tried to raise the money needed to build the enclosure and also the correct materials for the construction. The recession deepened, finances became tighter and the bank manager more unfriendly.

Spring turned to summer, although it was difficult to notice the change as the weather remained cold and wet. June temperatures were a record low, with sleet, hail and even snow replacing the expected summer sun. I began to despair of ever getting the animals' accommodation started, never mind completed. I considered withdrawing my offer to have the cats, but there was always that spark of hope. I desperately wanted them and couldn't bring myself to make the move that would deny me final access to them.

The Highland Wildlife Park contacted me in June to inquire if the enclosure was completed. Would I be collecting the cats that week? I explained my difficulties in finding the right wire mesh and reminded them that I had said August would be the earliest I could be ready. Even that date depended on the workmen being available.

The weeks sped by almost unnoticed, summer appeared briefly, and suddenly it was the end of August and still no work on the enclosure had begun despite a number of promises. The needed mesh was still proving difficult to obtain. The wildlife park phoned me again, and this time the tone was less than friendly. The cats had been moved to temporary accommodation and they wanted them rehoused quickly. It was all very well for them to say airily that the enclosure should have been finished – they had ready access to funds and materials and workmen on hand to carry out their projects, I had none of these on tap. Why couldn't they help with the construction? Jeremy Usher Smith was unsympathetic.

In October he informed me darkly that unless I had the accommodation ready in three weeks, he would make other arrangements for the two cats. I accepted that I had lost them but I still wanted to keep in touch with their whereabouts.

'Where will you send them?' I asked.

'Nowhere,' was the abrupt answer. 'It is not fair to keep the animals any longer in unsuitable accommodation, so I shall have to consider if they would be better off put down.'

Put down? I couldn't believe what I was hearing. Jeremy Usher Smith was calmly informing me that if I could not house the animals within three weeks, then they were to be destroyed . . . It was a cold, unemotional ultimatum – take them immediately or they are dead. They had kept the cats, both of which had been gifted to them, for three and six years yet they would not wait just a few weeks more.

I relayed the threat to Andrew Kitchener. He promised to attempt a stay of execution.

It seemed I needed a miracle to save the cats, and miracles have always been in short supply. Then I had a brainwave. I remembered TV personality Anneka Rice, who presented a programme that took on impossible challenges, persuading ordinary people to up tools and set about completing tasks with only goodwill and enthusiasm for the job as payment. Compared to the challenges the programme had undertaken, my little cat enclosure shrank to acceptable proportions. Sponsorship – that was what was needed, but could I copy Anneka and just ring round asking for help? A sort of mini-challenge? It was worth trying.

I grabbed the telephone directory and started to thumb through the yellow pages and increase my telephone bill. The first numbers I tried were the large oil companies in Aberdeen. Would anyone be willing, I asked, to provide either materials or manpower to help save such unique animals? Had I been wanting to house a shark or a whale I might have received more assistance – but cats? Well, there was no real publicity value to an oil company in the feline species, however rare. Some companies suggested I put my request in writing with promises they would be in touch in a few weeks. I did not have a few weeks. I tried the local distilleries, for surely the cats would be tourist attractions in the locality where they were living wild. It would be possible to set up a display of the history of the cats in one of their visitor centres in return for help, perhaps using one of the mounted specimens. I felt I had more to offer a distillery than an oil company. But most of those I called couldn't even be bothered to discuss the proposal.

'I'm afraid our charity donations are all spoken for,' said one woman coldly. 'Put your request in writing if you want to apply for next year.'

'The cats won't be alive in three weeks, never mind next year,' I informed the haughty voice, and gave up distilleries. The only one to be at all helpful was Glenfiddich who suggested that I call head office down south and speak to their director. It was Friday afternoon and the difficulty was that head office wouldn't be in action until the following week. With only three weeks to D-Day – death to cats day – time was running out. I tried Do-It-Yourself firms. If they could provide the materials free of charge, or even at cost, it would help, though not solve the problem completely. I was begining to admire Anneka Rice more and more, though of course she had all the power of television behind her.

The first Do-It-Yourself shop was a local firm but the owner was away for a week so that was a blank. The second, Texas, was another of the 'get in touch with head office next week', but with a difference. The lady to whom I spoke thought I might contact brigade RAF Kinloss as she knew that they had a squadron of engineers. That was something I hadn't even considered. If I could obtain the materials, who better than a team of service engineers to perform a speedy construction. After all, they were trained to build bridges, runways and even field hospitals in the middle of nowhere within hours rather than months. Surely a little cat enclosure would not defeat them?

My next call was to Magnet. The manager was very helpful but unfortunately the firm no longer handled building supplies, only windows, doors and fitted kitchens. He sounded genuinely sorry he was unable to assist, and I felt that a fitted kitchen was the last requirement for the cats, but he suggested a friend who owned a small up-and-coming building firm in Elgin.

'Give Graham Ferguson a ring. I'm sure he will be willing to help you.'

I did. By now I was running low on enthusiasm. 'I don't suppose you can help me, but . . .' I launched into the now familiar script and then paused, waiting for the usual polite refusal.

'I'm sure we can help,' said Graham Ferguson. 'Now what exactly do you need?'

I could scarcely believe it. All the giants that would not have noticed the cost had refused, and here was a small firm, which at a time of recession would have to watch its financial situation carefully, agreeing without any prevarication. I had a sponsor for the materials for the enclosure, now I needed manpower. I phoned Kinloss.

Hours later I was standing at the reception office of RAF Kinloss, waiting for the clerk to identify the officer I had arranged to see.

'I'm sorry, we don't appear to have a Warrant Officer Jones here at the camp,' said the young man apologetically.

'You must have,' I explained wearily. 'I was talking to him just a couple of hours ago and I've an appointment to see him.'

The young man shook his head, confused. 'I just can't find anyone of that name,' he said, peering at his computer screen. Other luckier people came and went, all able to trace their appointments. My WO Jones remained as elusive as the Morayshire mystery cats. Then an officer arrived to return some keys just as I gave a despairing wail that WO Jones must exist whether they could find him or not.

'Jones,' he said. 'You want Jones?' He nodded to the harassed clerk. 'He's army. You'll get him on 236 Field Squadron.'

I gushed my gratitude. The relieved clerk promptly rang the number and informed the elusive WO Jones that I had arrived.

'If you just wait in your car, madam, someone will come to escort you to the squadron.'

It was a longer wait than I'd expected but eventually I was on my way and discovering the reason for the delayed escort. WO Jones's office was about five miles into the camp. We trailed across runways with complicated lights flashing as planes screamed overhead, past massive hangers and through groups of assorted buildings. At last we arrived and I finally met WO Jones.

'I'll take you to meet my boss,' he said, and I was ushered into Colonel Hawkins' office. He was an elderly and kindly man and within minutes he was sketching out my requirements and working out what materials would be needed.

'Don't you worry, we'll have your cat cage built in no time,' he said, full of optimisim. 'I can't forsee any problems. We've three weeks, you say?'

'Less now,' I said. 'And getting hold of the right mesh is not easy.'

Colonel Hawkins shook his head. 'Oh, the wire won't be difficult. I'm sure we use something like it around the camp. If your builder has any problems getting hold of some, I'm sure we can trace enough for the purpose.'

Reassured, I pressed on to see Graham Ferguson in Elgin, armed with the squadron's promise of a construction team, a rough sketch of the cat's accommodation together and a list of materials needed.

Graham and his assistant Martin were equally optimistic. They would draw up the plans for the army to work with, provide the materials, even cutting the wood to size in their yard to facilitate an easier construction, and a home would be ready by the deadline to save the cats.

'Mesh? No problem!'

I went home feeling a great deal better and slept that night for the first time for days.

Alas, life is never smooth sailing, and even with Graham Ferguson's sponsorship and the military muscle, the cat enclosure was promised but not built. Kinloss was to launch a major military exercise the following week, promptly tying up all personnel in a mock war scenario. And my worst fears were realised – no one could get hold of the spot-welded mesh. It appeared it could only be obtained in England and no one seemed to know exactly where.

The days passed and became a week; still the manpower was playing wargames and the mesh was not forthcoming. I was seeing large-eyed whiskered faces in my sleep.

I talked to WO Jones, known to all as Q. 'Phone the Highland Wildlife Park,' he suggested. 'Tell them that we'll definitely get your enclosure built but we'll need a couple more weeks. They can't kill the cats for the sake of a few days, surely?'

The Highland Wildlife Park was resolute: sorry, you take the cats on the agreed date or not at all.

Andrew Kitchener rang me and I explained the situation. 'They won't mind a few days, surely?' was his response. 'Get the army to confirm that the cage will be built as agreed within a couple of weeks. The cats can't come to any harm left a couple of weeks more in their temporary home. I'll have a word with Jeremy.'

Andrew did. Afterwards he rang me again.

'Well?' I asked hopefully.

'He's very determined, isn't he?' Andrew said, his faith dwindling. Q tried as well. 'Not very helpful, are they?' was his verdict.

At least it wasn't just my poor powers of persuasion at fault. Between us we gained one day. I decided to notify the media of the cats' move, hoping that the publicity would persuade the wildlife park to give us a little more time. Grampian Television agreed to cover the rehousing of the animals as a news item.

That was all I could do. At last the military exercise was complete and the men came to see the site. They were to start work the following week. We had just five days to D-Day.

The carpenter, a pleasant young man named Gary, grinned. 'Oh, we'll get it up in no time, don't you worry.' He paused and I had a sinking feeling that all was not well. 'I can put the sleeping quarters and posts up, no problem. The only thing is . . .'

'Yes . . .?'

'We haven't been able to get the wire yet, but we've everything else. The wire just hasn't arrived.'

Five days to go and we hadn't got the wire for the run!

Gary and his helpers were true to their word. They trundled up the lane in a huge army truck piled high with wooden panels and posts. It took five men half a day to unload the already partly made-up shed. It was a giant jigsaw with huge wooden pieces to be fitted together on site. Trenches were hacked out of the rough ground and filled with quick setting concrete. Posts began to rise, walls were erected, roofs lowered, but, with three days to go, there was still no sign of the wire. Time had almost run out.

7

Two Bundles of Fury

The shed was constructed, the posts were deeply embedded in a concrete foundation, it was just one day to cat arrival day. I tried a last ditch play for extending the time limit by another couple of days but without success. The Highland Wildlife Park gave me until 10 a.m. on the Saturday when the vet would be on hand to give either the sedative for the journey or the lethal injection. I managed to get the collection time changed to 11 a.m. – one whole extra hour – but that was all.

On the Friday morning Gary and I surveyed the wooden framework and shed. John Deer, the local vet, was due to inspect the cats' new home and then phone through his approval to the Highland Wildlife Park before they would release their charges to my care. Grampian Television was also sending a crew to film the lads putting up the enclosure.

John arrived first, a little bemused about the whole affair. He examined the shed while we explained that the wire had yet to arrive.

'Just how wild are these cats?' he asked unhappily, displaying little enthusiasm for his potential new patients.

I shrugged. 'No one seems to know anything about them. According to the park staff, they are never seen in daylight.'

'What happens if one needs treatment? How do you intend to handle it?' He seemed to be disturbed by visions of us racing round the pen trying to grab the terrified feline by the scruff of the neck.

'I will have to construct a restrainer box.'

A restrainer box is a trap with sliding sides that enable the interior space to be made smaller, squashing the contained animal against the mesh without allowing it to turn and attack while it is sedated through the wire. It is a method of giving wild animals injections in the least stressful way possible, both for the patient and for the vet.

John looked relieved. 'That would be best,' he agreed. I said nothing about how we would persuade a reluctant cat to enter the box.

He passed the enclosure as suitable once the wire was in place and then phoned the Highland Wildlife Park to confirm that the cats would be housed adequately. He also inquired about their general condition and veterinary care.

I could hear only one side of the conversation but I think it was a call he regretted making. He looked pale as he murmured 'It could actually take a finger off?' I gained the impression that he fervently hoped the cats would remain in perfect health.

After John had gone, the TV crew arrived to film the lads finishing off the posts. They were also to film the actual move and arranged to meet me at the wildlife park at eleven o'clock the following day.

'We'd rather like some footage of the cats being shifted from their enclosure at the park,' said the cameraman thoughtfully.

'That you will have to arrange with them,' I told him, not giving a lot for his chances. Then they were gone and we were left to work in peace.

The structure was more or less complete except for the wire. Then I had an idea. George Watt, a local businessman, had used some spot-welded mesh for security fencing. He had told me he had a small amount left and if it would be of any use to me, I could have it. It wouldn't be enough to surround the enclosure, but it might just make a temporary wire front to the shed. We could put the cats in the smaller area just for the first couple of days and complete the surrounding pen while they remained in the shed. Providing, that is, that the wire George had left would be enough to seal off the shed entrance.

I jumped into the car and raced off to Keith. At first George had difficulty remembering where the wire mesh was, but a couple of phone calls finally located it.

'If it's any good, just help yourself,' he said.

I sped off to see just how much was left.

Almost a full roll of six-foot-high wire lay waiting for me. I gave a sigh of relief; it certainly looked enough to provide a temporary enclosure around the shed.

Within the hour it was being unrolled across my paddock and stapled into place. There wasn't enough daylight left to finish the job but by the time the wintry sun had set, the enclosure was partially meshed and suitable for the cats to be released into the following morning. Gary stood back and surveyed his handiwork unhappily.

'I wish we had a couple more days. I'm not at all satisfied with how it looks,' he muttered wearily.

'I think you've done a great job,' I said, relieved that we would make the deadline after so much uncertainty.

'There's really no chance we could put off collecting the cats for another couple of days?' he asked hopefully.

I shook my head. 'Not a chance. But everything is fine. We can keep them shut away in the shed until we complete the enclosure. They will be distressed by us working around them but at least they will still be alive!'

Gary nodded. 'I suppose so. I still haven't partitioned off the sleeping area.'

We had drawn up plans for dividing the interior of the shed into separate compartments that could provide different sleeping shelves and pens, enabling me to shut off the cats while I was cleaning out the main enclosure, and also to afford inner enclosures in case of sickness or indeed pregnancy. All we had managed to complete was the main structure of the shed and one large sleeping shelf. Time and the light had run out, but at least we had somewhere to put the two cats when I collected them the following morning.

My car wasn't large enough to carry their travelling boxes so Graham Ferguson once again stepped into the breach and offered the use of his van. When next morning he and Martin failed to arrive on time, I started to panic. If we were just a few minutes late, the wildlife park might carry out its threat and top the cats.

Graham laughed reassuringly when finally he turned up to collect me. 'Don't worry, we've plenty of time,' he said cheerfully.

'But it takes about two hours from here.'

'Not the way he drives,' said Martin darkly.

It was a nerve-racking drive but, true to his word, Graham swung into the entrance to the wildlife park just before the deadline of eleven. I looked round the deserted car park for the television crew but they were not to be seen. Graham turned up the track and drove through the park to the now familiar office buildings. There was no sign of the television crew at the office block either, but Jeremy Usher Smith was waiting with the cats, boxed and ready. I signed the release papers, was given their medical history charts, and we loaded the two boxes containing the cats into the van. I still couldn't see them as the mesh fronts of the boxes were covered with sacking to keep the animals in darkness. They had not been sedated for the journey, but apart from the odd growl they seemed quiet enough.

Then we were off home. We rattled around the bend, swung out of the park entrance and let out a cheer. Mission cat accomplished! Whatever the cats were, they were alive.

And they were mine.

There was still no sign of the TV crew. I presumed that either they were not coming or would go directly to the house. Our journey back was a good deal slower than our journey there, none of us fancying the idea of a pile up, especially with the vision of the cat boxes smashing open, releasing their irate unsedated prisoners in the cramped confines of the van.

Two hours later we were home and my young lodger Mandy met me at the door.

'The TV man's been phoning. They've been waiting at the park since eleven but they must have missed you. They're on the way over and said don't release the cats till they get here!'

We discovered later that the television crew had arrived just minutes after us, but instead of driving up the lane to the offices, they had parked in the deserted car park near the closed ticket box and waited out of sight of us as we returned along the track and headed home.

While awaiting the lost crew, Graham and Martin had a look at the incomplete pen.

'Might as well spend our time making this wire more secure,' Graham said, pointing to the various small gaps where the roof and sides did not quite meet. I left them hammering away and went back to the van where the two cats were still in their travelling boxes. The male was in a wooden crate with only a narrow mesh panel beneath the sacking. It was too dark to see the animal and the only result of moving the sacking was a furious growl and a loud pistol shot, *Phaah*! I decided to leave well alone and turned to the other cat. She was in a carrying box with a wire mesh door like a giant cat basket. I lifted the sacking, allowing a shaft of daylight to enter and stared once again at the *Tomorrow's World* cat. The first time I had seen only the head; now I could see the whole body. I stared in amazement. Eddie Orbell at the park had told me she was no more than a black domestic cat. Certainly she was small for a Kellas, with a slightly longer tail, so perhaps was not true to type, but otherwise she was exactly like the other specimens. Her black fur had long white guard hairs scattered throughout it. There was a small white star on her chest, her tail was bushy, her body long and lean. She stared at me from burning orange eyes and snarled, revealing large white teeth.

PHAAH!

Instinctively I flinched as she struck out, even the heavy mesh separating us seeming inadequate protection from her razor claws. I sat beside the cage and talked softly to her, keeping my voice low and even, attempting to reassure her. After a few minutes she settled back and watched me curiously, her eyes strangely blank, as if hooded to hide her thoughts. I could hardly credit it. If the male was a Kellas, then I had a pair! The *Tomorrow's World* team had caught a Kellas, or a hybrid Kellas; this was not a domestic feral as I'd been told.

At that moment the missing TV crew arrived with the Grampian presenter Donald John MacDonald and I had to tear myself away from studying the *Tomorrow's World* Kellas.

The enclosure was looking a lot more secure, only the odd small gap visible under the roof where the wire did not quite meet. Even the presenter gave a hand with the last staples. Then it was time to release the cats before the light failed, preventing filming.

With the cameraman trailing after me, I took the two carrying boxes into the enclosure and shut the gate. I was now locked in with the cats and one had to be released before the other, meaning that I had to be in the enclosure with one cat running loose while I let the other free and then made a quick exit. Had the cats been sedated, there would have been no problem, but the cats had not been sedated, and they were wide awake, alert, angry and frightened. One could not expect them to be in a happy or friendly frame of mind having been boxed for at least three hours, bundled into the van and bounced and bumped across the Grampian Mountains. I wondered if the cameraman was going to get a bigger story than he expected.

Nervously I decided to release the female first. She had been in captivity longest and was also smaller, so I hoped she would be less likely to attack. I remembered the park's final instruction to me: 'Keep your hands out of the way when you undo the catch; she'll have your finger off if she gets the chance.' I hadn't noticed any keepers short of fingers, but they seemed rather obsessed by the finger risk.

It was not easy to release the catch without my hands making contact with the door, but finally, with all fingers still attached to the hand, I succeeded and, thrusting the box in front of me, I tipped it up. Nothing happened. I shook it. Still nothing. Conscious of the camera whirring, I shook the box frantically. At last a flash of black emerged growling furiously and the female shot out of the box to spin round in panic in the centre of the pen. For a fraction of a second she assessed the situation, her eyes darting from side to side, then without hesitation she sprang for one of the support posts and shot up it, straight for one of the suspect gaps. Everyone spotted her intention and rushed round the outside to block her route. Screaming in anger, she leapt across the mesh for another tiny gap. All outside watchers raced round to head her off, shouting and waving their arms, the cameraman almost getting trampled in the rush. The presenter and the soundman joined in the fun with enthusiasm. The cat made two more attempts at escape, her speed of calculation revealing an amazing intelligence. I stood frozen, my back to the locked door, the male, still boxed on the ground beside me while the spitting bundle of fury raced around the enclosure. Then the totally unexpected happened. I had hoped she would seek shelter in the shed and didn't expect her to run straight at me, spitting and hissing her anger. As I prepared for her to launch at me, she raced past to take cover between my legs, the door and the male's box. There she crouched growling, her tail lashing from side to side, her eyes blazing hatred at the faces staring in at her. She was actually pressed against the backs of my legs!

Time seemed to stand still. I spoke quietly.

'Please don't anyone move or make a sound. Stay absolutely still.'

Luckily everyone recognised the danger I was in and, like a Simon Said children's game, everyone froze. So did the cat. I could feel the vibrations of her growls against my skin and

I knew that the slightest provocation would have her lashing out to rip my flesh to shreds. She was small, not much bigger than a domestic cat, but she had vicious claws that could cut like razor blades into my unprotected bare legs. I remained motionless, so did the cat. I waited. She wriggled in even tighter, swearing and spitting at the watchers beyond the wire, seeming to be unconscious of my presence or else not counting me as a danger to her. Not a bad assessment of the situation.

After a few minutes, I could not hold the position without moving, so very slowly, inch by inch, I began to ease myself away from the snarling animal. At any moment I expected to feel the hot tearing pain of her claws making contact with my flesh, but she continued to ignore me and concentrated her venom on those who were preventing her escape. Then I was clear. On finding her cover gone, she reared up and with a final *Phaah!* made for the doorway of the shed and disappeared into the darkness to bury herself in the straw beneath the sleeping shelf.

I was conscious of my legs trembling with the strain of remaining so still and the shock of the incident. I still had to deal with the bigger male cat and was not enjoying myself, aware of the camera whirring nearby, filming every movement. I forced myself to remain calm and, leaning forward, I threw open the male's box and leapt back, this time expecting the unexpected. Nothing happened. I shook the box. The only result was an infuriated *Phaah!* I shook harder. Still no cat emerged. I threw caution to the wind and almost tipped the box upside down. Still the cat didn't appear. I became desperate and bent over to peer inside. The cat stared back at me, spitting furiously, all four paws stretched out to anchor it, the claws embedded deeply into the wooden sides of the box. He was hanging on for grim death and nothing I could do was going to dislodge him. I shook the box hard and turned it completely upside down. Gravity took over and before anyone could blink, a black streak headed for the safety of the shed and the straw.

It was over. The cameraman stopped filming and I was let out of the enclosure.

After so long, I still hadn't seen the Ross-shire cat! Neither had the cameraman, for in the split second it had taken the creature to cross the pen, he had switched off the camera, thinking nothing was happening for a moment. The cat that hadn't been filmed or photographed since its capture had escaped the camera again.

But if I still couldn't be sure that the Ross-shire feline was a Kellas, I retracted all I had said over the years about the *Tomorrow's World* cat. Martin Hughes-Games might have produced a lousy and misleading programme but it appeared he had caught a Kellas after all.

The next day I spent a good deal of my time sitting by the mesh, talking softly to the shed doorway. The two cats had found their way to the sleeping shelf where they crouched embedded in the straw, only their backs visible, two dark humps from which emitted terrifying snarls and the loud pistol shot spits that made me jump feet every time I heard them.

I had saved the cats, they were housed, even if the enclosure wasn't complete, but I was now faced with a new problem. The Highland Wildlife Park had fed them only with rabbits and the occasional trout from a local fish farm. I did not have access to an unlimited supply of either commodity, so the rabbit hunt began in earnest. I had stockpiled a few, but I hoped to persuade the cats to try a more easily obtainable menu.

On the following Monday, Gary arrived and so at last did the promised wire. It took two days more to complete and secure the enclosure around the shed as we were being doubly cautious. The female's escape bids had shown us that we dare not miss so much as a loose staple anywhere. Her reticence and anger I had been prepared for, but not her intelligence.

By Wednesday it was finished and the temporary panel was removed from the shed doorway, giving the cats access to the whole pen. We cracked a bottle of champagne for lunch to celebrate, then with my thanks ringing in their ears, the army volunteers in their vehicles bumped and crashed away up the potholed lane.

Operation Save Cat was completed, now Operation Breed Cat was about to begin.

Before that, however, came Operation Feed Cat.

8

Attack and Counter-attack

For the first few days the two cats remained on their sleeping shelf during the short winter daylight hours, the female crouched so low she was almost completely hidden, but the bigger male was easier to see, rearing up and giving a full display of aggression, snarling and spitting the moment anyone approached the enclosure. Even so, it was difficult to see him clearly in the gloom, but I had no doubt he was a full Kellas, whatever they were. He was very large, twice the size of the female, with a small head, a long powerful muscular body and very short clubbed bushy tail. As soon as I went near the enclosure he would crouch low, his back arched, then suddenly spring forward as though about to launch himself, feinting an attack with a loud furious *PHAAH*!

Every day I put a pair of dead rabbits into the enclosure and by next morning they had always been carried into the shed and partly buried under the sleeping shelf. It was impossible to be certain how much was being eaten and two rabbits a day meant fourteen rabbits a week, the demand definitely outstripping the supply. So desperate was I that even the postman dropped off a fresh road casualty. I tried other tasty titbits. Chickens, easy to obtain as natural wastage from chicken farms, were turned down immediately. A goose that had died of natural causes was shoved into the pen to be stored and ignored.

The abandoned food was also a problem. Everything offered was promptly carried into the shed and dumped under the sleeping shelf during the night. The bedding straw was constantly raked over the whole decomposing mess. With the male constantly alert and on guard, there was no way I could enter the shed to find out how much was being eaten. Three or four times a day I entered the enclosure and stood or crouched in the shed entrance, talking softly, trying to accustom the cats to my scent and voice. The female remained hidden at the rear of the shelf but the male always rose up and lashed out in a quite terrifying manner. He was a magnificent beast, his orange-gold eyes burning with hatred for his captors as he struck out with large heavily clawed paws, spitting with the typical wildcat abrupt, loud and penetrating *Phaah*!

Within the first few days he had earned the name Freddy after the central character Freddy Kruger in the horror film *Nightmare on Elm Street*. It was a name he worked hard to live up to to. His unsociable mate became Freda.

Fred's attacks continued unabated, but there was a subtle difference. He still greeted me with screaming fury, but the blazing hatred in the eyes grew less evident and after his macho display he would settle back and watch me curiously, as if waiting for me to make the next move. Neither cat attempted to leave the shelter of the shelf in daylight. Exactly a week after their arrival I was feeding the peacock when I glanced across to the cat enclosure to see Fred crouched in the shed doorway, watching me. The moment he realised he had been spotted, he turned and fled back into the safety of the shed.

The next evening Fred was crouched on the step of the enclosure, studying me feeding the birds. I turned to face him across the paddock and he held his ground until I walked towards him. The following evening he was seated outside in the enclosure for the first time. He watched me intently but held his ground as I approached to feed them. He snarled and spat as I reached the pen and retreated to the doorway, even though I was less than four feet from him. It was the first real chance I had had to study him. He was a beautiful creature, his black coat gleaming in the fading light. The single white hairs on his flanks shining with an opalescent glow. His eyes blazed, their golden depths reflecting the setting sun. A fairy cat, etheral, erie, a ghost from the past.

He snarled and spat loudly, pulling his head back and jerking forward as though actually hurling the *Phaah*! at me. I flinched. It was a violent sound that made one involuntarily pull back. I kept talking softly as I put the rabbits into the pen, bracing myself for a fast exit, but although he continued to voice his displeasure in no uncertain terms, he made no attempt to attack.

I moved slowly out of the pen and secured the two gates quietly. He remained seated, watching me intently as I walked away.

In less than two weeks Fred appeared to have accepted my presence. I was elated.

The next few days followed the same pattern. Both cats remained hidden in the straw of the sleeping shelf during the day, although any approach to the enclosure brought an immediate and violent response from Fred. At dusk the big male was prowling the pen, waiting for his supper, as I arrived with my offerings of rabbits. He always remained in the shed entrance when I entered the pen, spitting and snarling his warning, but the displays were less violent. If anyone else approached, he immediately went into his former glory of screaming fury and loud pistol shot *Phaah*'s. There was a marked difference in his reaction towards me and to strangers.

If the male was willing to accept my presence on his terms, Freda was still keeping a low profile. I never saw her other than as a hissing hump buried in the straw. I also noticed that the floor of the pen and the shed was never fouled after their night's activities. There was no evidence of digging in the ground of the enclosure but the piles of straw under the shelf were pulled about and rearranged on a nightly basis. I concluded that one pile of straw was a food store and another was the latrine area. It suggested that in the wild the cats had scraped loose debris, such as grass and leaves, over their droppings but did not dig holes like a domestic cat.

It was also puzzling that there was no evidence of Fred scent-marking his territorial boundaries. Most tom-cats urinate at chosen points around their territory to show other cats their boundaries. Wildcats actually leave exposed droppings for presumably the same purpose. The first sign of acceptance of their new home by the Kellas cats should have been scent-marking. However the enclosure remained spotlessly clean, only the constantly rearranged piles of straw suggesting their toilet activities. I reported back to Andrew Kitchener who was surprised and suggested that maybe I had missed the signs. But I hadn't: there was no evidence of spray marks on the wood of the shed, or on posts, and no droppings, buried or otherwise, around the perimeter of the wire. There was also no smell, something else I found surprising as most cat species emit a strong pungent smell from their scent glands.

Feeding became no easier as time passed. Spring and summer provide an abundance of rabbits in the countryside, but autumn and especially winter with its lack of vegetation sees a natural culling of the creatures, survivors being seldom seen until the fresh green grass appears with the arrival of young in spring. It was winter and my supply of rabbits was quickly drying up. I tried various other foods and finally the two cats accepted rabbit-size strips of beef and pork although they rejected lamb – a source of comfort to local farmers, no doubt. Whatever else the wild Kellas cats endangered on farms, sheep appeared safe from their predatory habits.

With my attempts to vary their diet came the difficulty of removing anything that was refused yet still carted into the food store. Because of the lack of time to complete the enclosure, I had no way of partitioning off part of the shed so that I could have access for cleaning while the cats were shut out. Two cats permanently on guard and displaying extreme aggression in the defence of their territory effectively ensured that I did not cross the boundary and enter the shed. I was tolerated in the enclosure because I provided food, but I never pushed my luck by overstepping the mark. Always I was under close scrutiny, my every movement keenly studied. If either cat felt threatened by me, then I had little doubt that a full frontal attack would be launched in earnest, and as the sleeping shelf was chest height, such an attack in an enclosed space would cause considerable damage. It was essential to be restrained and constantly alert.

The goose remained uneaten for two weeks before suddenly one morning the pen was full of feathers and the bird carcase torn apart. It appeared that the cats had not actually rejected it but they liked their goose gamey.

Although keeping the cats secluded and away from people, I did allow an occasional visitor to approach the pen and peer across through the open door of the shed to where the cats could be seen on their shelf. Fred always greeted such liberties by rearing up and striking out with his front feet like a challenging stallion, then stamping down hard with pistol shot spits and deep throaty snarling. Freda seldom put on a display for intruders. She remained hidden in the straw, only the black arch of her back in view.

Every day I entered the enclosure three or four times, once to put in the evening feed but the others just to stand in the shed entrance and talk softly to the cats, wanting them to become used to the sound and scent of me in the hope that they would eventually accept and trust me. Fred began to appear in the enclosure at feeding times, watching me feed the other animals and complete my evening chores before finally bringing the cats their meat. As soon as I approached, he would turn and disappear into the gloom of his shed. He would stand in the entrance growling softly but not spitting. He appeared to have accepted my presence but I was being warned not to push my luck. I felt the breakthrough had been made one evening when he sat quietly watching me fill his water dish without even a token snarl, his eyes bright and interested, watching my every move. I moved quietly and quickly, ignoring him as he studied me.

A couple of days later he did not even retreat to the shed but remained in the enclosure, crouched ready for instant flight or attack but standing his ground. After that he never retreated at my approach and spent more and more time out of the shed during daylight hours. Any approach by anyone else and he would flee to the security of the shelter where he would exbibit the full wildcat warning display. While Freda remained hidden, he would stand very upright, stretched to his full height, his back arched, hair erect, but his rear crouched, swinging slightly as if preparing to pounce. He would snarl and growl throatily, punctuated by the pistol shot spits, his eyes blazing hatred. His *Phaah*! was always accompanied by a jerk backwards almost as if he were recoiling from the abrupt sound.

When I was alone he still growled and snarled a warning but he remained in a more relaxed upright position, his back arched and his rear shuffling as though considering a swing. The greatest change however was in the eyes; he still stared wide-eyed but there was no longer the maniacal stare. After a few minutes with me talking softly, he would visibly relax. Although still snarling, he would blink, sometimes actually closing his eyes for a few moments as though resting. His fury towards me seemed purely token although I always had the impression that one false move would provoke an instant attack.

On New Year's Eve I was a little later feeding the animals than usual. Fred was waiting as I entered the enclosure, and he came to meet me. It was the first time he had ever actually approached me. He gave a loud *Phaah*, to express his displeasure at my bad timekeeping, then retreated to the shed entrance where he behaved in a very agitated manner, shaking his head, repeatedly half-sitting and then standing and scratching his ear. Then he came away from the shed and approached me again, growling. I was worried that he might have toothache or earache, although I hoped his behaviour was simply because he had been kept waiting for his food. Freda was completely out of sight and I wondered if anything had happened to her. Had she died in the straw, or even produced kittens? It was a very windy night, a howling gale blowing around the sleet, so I hoped she had just burrowed into the straw for comfort. There was no way I could enter the shed to find out.

At first light I checked the pen to discover that there had been considerable activity during the night. The floor straw had been thoroughly rooted through and pulled away from the wall into new heaps with straw-covered chunks of stored meat dragged to the centre of the shed. Freda was visible, crouched on the shelf, and to my relief both cats appeared to be behaving normally. I had spent Hogmanay wondering how I was going to treat either of them if anything were wrong. At the evening feed Fred produced his usual half-hearted display and gave no sign that anything was the matter.

A couple of days later I was surprised on my morning visit to see Fred crouched in Freda's usual place on the sleeping shelf. At my approach he stood up for his normal macho display and his mate slipped quickly back into her regular place behind him. Immediately he swung round and attacked her, driving her back along the shelf before settling himself, snarling, back into her favoured spot. She reared up and fought back, but she was no match for the massive tom and she retreated miserably, obeying his command. It was the first time I had seen any communication between them and I wondered if it were a prelude to mating behaviour or just bloody-mindedness on Fred's behalf. Freda glared at me and spat loudly as if the whole episode had been my fault.

The food store had again been rummaged through and I suspected the change in the relationship between the two cats could be connected with the apparent house cleaning. Was it part of courtship? Perhaps he was finding the choicest chunk of stored meat to offer her as a delicacy.

The next day I glanced up while feeding the birds in the morning and saw both cats out in the enclosure, watching me. It was the first time I had had the chance to compare the pair, Freda was only half the size of the male. The moment she realised she had been observed, she fled back to the safety of the shed, moving in a crouched position, her belly close to the ground.

That afternoon I took fresh straw into the pen for their latrine heap as they were now always using the one tidy heap of straw in the enclosure. Fred investigated the fresh heap, digging into it and then rearing back in a nervous movement. Finally he sat beside the pile, studying it intently as if expecting it to do something interesting. He remained in the enclosure all day, patrolling the wire and spitting softly whenever approached. His whole behaviour was different from normal.

The following morning Freda was again out in the enclosure, although she dashed inside as soon as she spotted me. For the following few days Fred remained unusually active. The weather was becoming colder and I decided to attempt to change their accommodation to more comfortable quarters. I used a solid Victorian chest of drawers from which to construct a small portable den. I left in the lower deep drawer, but removed the upper ones, boarding in the front with a framed entrance. I added a drop down sliding door that could be operated by means of a cord and then covered the entire top with roofing compound. Stuffed with straw, it made a waterproof warm and cosy den, even if its outward appearance was a little rough.

Making it was one thing; getting it into the den was another. The cats were both showing extremely aggressive behaviour, Fred was always in the enclosure with me, never in the shed, and he was showing distinct signs of considering an attack. He would semi-crouch, his rear swinging from side to side, his tail lashing slowly as he made forward jerks as if about to launch, then pull back, growling. He had also begun to rush at the bars with a furious *Phaah*! every time he spotted anyone near the enclosure. Entering the pen with my back towards him, dragging a heavy chest of drawers, was an altogether different proposition from facing him with offerings of meat.

I decided to take some precautions. I chose a day of pouring rain, knowing that the cats would be sheltering in the shed. I also dressed in copious layers of clothing in the hope of deflecting any teeth and claws aimed in my direction and I borrowed a full face motorbike helmet. Then I was ready. Mandy helped me to carry the chest across the garden to the cats' enclosure, the rest of the livestock looking rather bemused by the waddling vision I had become. I intended to open the inner door and heave the chest through, Mandy slamming the outer door shut the moment it was clear.

I did not know until I tried it that the army lads had spilt concrete in the passageway and this prevented the inner door opening fully. We had lugged the chest silently into position through the icy downpour, hoping the rain would drown out any sounds we made. Quietly I opened the outer door and we engineered the chest into the opening. There was no room for manoeuvering. I stood jammed between the chest and the inner door. So far, so good; we had not disturbed the cats. I unlatched the inner door with freezing hands and attempted to pull it open quickly. The bottom of the door hit a concrete hump with a bang that vibrated through me and rattled my teeth. Immediately there was an echoing crash from the shed as Fred hit the floor on his way to investigate the unexpected activity. There was a furious *Phaah*! as he skidded to the door just as I slammed it shut. Silence and stealth was a thing of the past. With Fred leaping and swearing at the upper mesh of the door, his huge clawed paws reaching through, groping to try and hook me, I hammered and chipped at the concrete until it was level enough to allow the door to clear. Then we dragged the chest outside the enclosure and retreated back to the house to dry out and warm up.

A couple of hours later, we tried again. This time the door opened but as I dragged the chest through, it jammed in the doorway, leaving me trapped in the enclosure with a snarling Fred studying me from the shed. The chest was so tight fitting that I had to wriggle and heave it through inch by inch. At least Mandy was able to slam the outer door closed, but with the chest stuck I had no means of a quick exit. I was fearfully conscious of having my back turned towards the cat just three feet from me, but I had no choice. To get the chest through I had to concentrate on the task in hand and ignore Fred watching the whole procedure with curious eyes. It was getting dark before the new den was in position and I was once more safely outside the enclosure. I went to get the evening feed. When I returned, Fred was already investigating his new furnishing, sniffing it and standing on his hindlegs to peer inside. In the confusion I had not noticed my Great Dane following me from the house. I had always been careful to keep the other animals away from the cat enclosure, but there was nothing I could do. She came loping up to the wire, obviously delighted to greet the strangers. It was the first time Fred had seen one of the dogs, and he stood shocked as she bent down to sniff the wire, her huge nose quivering. He stared for a moment, then without hesitation strode stiff-legged and arrogantly across to meet her. I shouted the dog away, amazed by the cat's laid back attitude. I fed the cats and finished for the day.

At first light, I went to see if the cats had investigated the new den. The straw was beaten down in the entrance so obviously they had looked inside. I checked the shed. For the first time the shelf was empty. Both cats were comfortably dug into their new den. Fred's face appeared framed in the doorway with a warning growl. I'd given him his new home and I sure as hell wasn't going to get it back!

The next few days showed a change in Fred's behaviour. Up until then I had been allowed in the enclosure but not in the shed. Now he was showing distinct territorial behaviour about the enclosure as well, attacking the mesh as soon as he spotted me. Even when I was bringing rabbits that had to be dropped inside the pen, he began to attack the door, leaping at the wire, his massive paws hooking through in vicious swipes. I began posting the smaller chunks of meat through the wire as a safety precaution. As he lost his fear of me so he had become more dangerous. But he was now easy to study, which after all was part of the project. Although my ultimate aim was to breed them, it might not be possible, owing to their age or fertility, so studying their behaviour was the secondary aim.

As the weeks passed, so I was able to observe Fred on a daily basis, while Freda was glimpsed only occasionally. Then one day Freda did not flee at the sight of me, but held her ground, crouched low, spitting warnings. Fred threw himself at the wire with a loud *Phaah!* I decided we were not going through all that again, so I dropped down on my knees and gave a reasonably good imitation of his spit. He jerked back, startled, and stared at me in shock. I growled and he sat back, his confidence clearly shaken.

The next morning was bitterly cold with a coating of thick ice everywhere. The cats were nowhere to be seen. At feeding time both were seated side by side on the top of their new den, watching for me coming from their newly discovered vantage point. Freda shot to the safety of the shed when I arrived but Fred launched his usual attack on the wire. I ignored the display and dropped the meat into the enclosure before going back to the house for hot water to melt the ice in their water bowl. He pranced backwards and forwards, feinting and attacking, growling and snarling. I growled back and he flinched before launching another attack. When I returned with the water he was crouched in the centre of the enclosure with his back towards me, eating. I poured the water into the bowl and he spun round, realising for the first time I was there, and rushed to attack. I stamped and growled and he retreated slightly. He sank back and studied me intently. Was I really daring to challenge him? Then he spotted a chicken walking past the pen. He promptly ignored me and began to stalk the bird, pouncing suddenly, only the mesh saving the bird's life.

It was obvious that, despite his captive years, his hunting instinct was as strong as ever. He might have been changing his behaviour towards humans, but chickens were still fair game. But then the chickens were unlikely to return his challenge.

9

Uneasy Truce

If Fred was becoming slightly over-confident, the same could not be said for Freda, who was definitely of the shy retiring type. Then one day I caught her out in the enclosure at feeding time. Instead of the usual frantic dash for the safety of her sleeping den, she stood her ground, snarling and spitting from the shelter of Fred's tail. I dropped the meat in and Fred lunged forward to throw himself at the bars in his usual friendly manner, claws extended as his paws reached through the mesh to lash at me. Satisfied that his honour was held intact by his display of ingratitude, he dropped down, inspected the meat, chose his first chunk and, grabbing it with a growl, turned and walked stiff-legged to the hut.

Suddenly Freda's shelter was gone and she stood exposed to my gaze, unprotected by the more powerful aggressive tom. She was horrified, spitting and snarling as she crouched low, her bright eyes darting from me to the distant safety of her den. But she also wanted the food, it was there in front of her, chunks of glistening bloody meat. Her nose wrinkled and her bright red tongue curled to lick her lips.

I stayed motionless. Would she trust me enough to approach for her supper?

She was terrified of me, but her greed was stronger than her fear, she sank down on her belly and slowly inched her way

116

forward, closer and closer to her quarry, snarling and growling, her large golden eyes never leaving my face for an instant, ready for a speedy retreat if I showed any sign of movement. She reached the meat – and a dilemma. To get the meat, she had to take her eyes off me. She froze, undecided; the rich scent of the bloody chunks was right under her curling lip. She could smell it, taste it. She wanted it! It was worth the risk. She dropped her gaze, grabbed the nearest piece and in a blur of movement, turned to dash for her den and disappeared into the darkness. I still made no movement. Her face appeared, framed in the opening, and she bravely spat *Phaah*! She had beaten me. She'd dared and won!

I left her to her hard earned meal.

The following evening, Fred was waiting as usual, licking his chops in anticipation of both his evening meal and his nightly attack on me, I was never sure which he enjoyed the most. Behind him Freda crouched snarling, brave with new found courage. Fred sprang forward, gave me a blast of the verbal and a couple of quick token swipes before taking his choice bit of meat and making off with it to his feeding shelf in the shed. She remained uncertain, her courage almost deserting her on finding herself alone with me. Again her eyes darted towards the safety of her den, but the scent of the meat was irresistible. She dashed forward, grabbed the nearest chunk and was away, her tail fluffed out as she disappeared through the entrance into the security of the sheltered darkness of her den.

On the third night she still waited her turn, Fred, as the dominant male, always got first choice, but she now took time to inspect the remaining three pieces, choosing carefully although her eyes never left me for more than a fraction of a second.

During the next morning's feeding of the other animals not only Fred sat in the enclosure studying my movements, Freda sat by his side, watching me feed the old ewe and the birds, though I was unsure whether it was me or the proximity of all the fat juicy geese and hens that aroused her interest.

I finished feeding and glanced back at the enclosure. The cats were still sitting bolt upright, ears pricked, studying the scene intently. I wondered if Freda would stand her ground without the lure of the meat. I walked slowly across, expecting her to make her usual headlong dash for cover on being caught out in the open. She glanced a couple of times towards her den, but she held her ground, spitting and snarling, her eyes blazing hatred as she gave a miniature edition of Fred's usual display of contained ferocity. She did not spring at the wire like her larger more powerful mate, but she gave a couple of token lunges to warn me that, although she appeared to be accepting my presence, peace was still not being declared between us. It was the first breakthrough in a form of relationship with her.

I remained still, talking softly to both cats, ignoring Fred's unsociable assaults on the wire, while she remained crouched behind him, snarling and hissing. There was no food in front of her this time to hold her attention and provide an incentive to remain in the danger zone, so she was staying because of her newfound confidence.

Then suddenly the unexpected happened. Fred abandoned his attack on me, spun round and lashed out at Freda. She responded by rising up on to her hind legs and lashing back at him, claws extended as they exchanged blows, but she was no match for the massive Tom. With a parting *Phaah*!, she turned tail and retreated to the sleeping pen, leaving Fred to turn back to resume his attack on me.

I was surprised at the sudden turn of events and puzzled by the meaning of it. Had Fred decided that his mate should not remain in the danger area and so had chased her back into the safety of the den, or had it been a form of jealousy? Was he keeping her away because he considered I was his property alone and he was not not going to allow her to muscle in on his territory?

Whatever the reason for his violent attack on her, I left him to his hollow victory, walking away, and abandoning him to the isolation of his choice.

13 Three Kellas kittens venture out of the den box for the first time, probably at about four weeks old.

14 The kit's father, Fred, looks aloof and shows no aggression.

15 The kits explore with their mother, Freda.

16   Freda moved the kitten back to safety by grabbing the tiny creature in her mouth.

17   The kittens basking in the sun on top of the den box in which they were secretly and silently reared from birth.

18, 19 By eight weeks the kittens' striped coats started to turn chocolate brown and blue eyes to green and then gold.

20 Freda protected the kits with a fierce display at any sign of approach by humans.

21 Fred staring into the neighbouring pen of the three-legged female.

22   At three months the kits sun themselves on the den box.

23   Although remaining fierce, Fred was no longer dominant once the kittens arrived.

24   Freda feeding the kits at about three months old.

Despite the unexpected ending to the encounter, I was elated. I was certain the week had provided the first signs of a breakthrough in Freda's behaviour. According to the Highland Wildlife Park, she had never shown any wish to have any form of relationship with man, avoiding any such encounter. Within three months of being in my care, she was showing signs of accepting an uneasy truce and in fact she seemed to be rushing through the first stages of the relationship, unlike Fred who had taken weeks to reach the point where he would voluntarily remain in my presence.

It seemed that, if nothing happened to upset the routine – and I played it quietly and calmly – then within days, or at the most, a couple of weeks. I would be able to see her regularly and gauge her physical condition. This was important because it would enable me to detect the first signs of pregnancy and give me a chance to separate her from Fred in the hope of keeping the kittens alive. How I was going to achieve the separation remained a mystery, but if I could see a spreading girth, I could at least plan ahead for the coming event. Provided, of course, nothing happened to upset the routine.

That day I came home at lunchtime to find my answer phone flashing. Colin Barclay, the game keeper at Kellas, wanted me to call him. I knew he intended to come over to see the cats in captivity and I presumed, as I hadn't seen him for some months, that was the reason for his call. I made a sandwich for lunch and, slurping a cup of coffee, I rang his number, starting the conversation with the usual polite chit chat about his family and the weather. Then he said calmly, almost as an afterthought:

'Oh, by the way, I trapped another Kellas cat this morning. Do you want it?'

'Yes please!' It had been a couple of years since the last Kellas had been killed so a fresh carcase was going to be welcomed by the museum staff. Then I remembered my over crammed freezer. There was nowhere to put another body. 'Er, could you keep it for me?' I asked. 'I've no room in the freezer.'

'This one's alive,' said Colin cheerfully.

'Alive!'

'But I'm afraid it's badly injured. I think it'll have to have a paw amputated and it's lost its front teeth trying to smash its way out of the trap,' Colin added. 'If it had been a feral cat or a fox I would have shot it immediately, but as soon as I saw it was a Kellas I put it in a sack to keep for you. Its extremely ferocious and it would have done itself even more damage if I'd left it in the trap.'

I was stunned. The elation would come later; first there was panic. I knew better than most just how ferocious the animals were. Even injured, it wasn't going to be an animal I could put in a cardboard box to recover by my bedside. It wouldn't even be possible to examine it without completely sedating it. Yet, whatever the difficulties, if it could be saved, it had to be. Only two other Kellas cats had been captured alive in eight years. If the new cat was a Kellas, then it had to be treated urgently and accomodated to help counter the shock it would be suffering. My mind raced, trying to decide what course of action to take.

'How is the cat now?' I asked.

'Quiet,' said Colin. 'It's remaining calm and quiet in the sack. As luck would have it, I'm coming over your way tonight. If you like, I'll drop it in to you.'

'Fine. How badly injured is it?'

'I don't think you will save its front paw which looks pretty mangled. Otherwise it seems in pretty good shape, though obviously I couldn't get more than a brief glimpse of it. I felt it best to get it bagged and out of the trap as quickly as possible before it did any more damage to itself.'

While he'd been speaking, I'd had time to consider the situation. 'I think we need to get it to a vet as quickly as possible,' I said. 'Look, I'll give Brian Smedley a ring to see if there's any chance of borrowing a cage until I can get an enclosure built. I'll also ring the vet to ask him to have a look at it urgently. I'll ring you back.' I put down the phone and dialled the SSPCA officer only to be greeted by an answer phone and the information that he was out and about and his mobile car number if it was an emergency. An injured Kellas in a sack, I decided, was definitely an emergency so I dialled the car number. Brian answered and I explained the situation.

'Where is the cat?' he asked. I told him. 'I'm not far from there. Would you like me to pick it up for you, I've a carrying box in the van.'

Considering his area covered a few hundred square miles, it was pure luck he was within a few minutes' drive of the Kellas estate when I contacted him.

I said I would tell Colin to expect him and then arrange for the vet to be on standby as soon as we could get the cat to the surgery. Then it would be a case of waiting to find out how badly injured the cat was – and its sex.

It was a fairly safe bet that it would be another male as three quarters of the Kellas cats killed were male.

A couple of hours after my phone call to Colin, I stood with Brian Smedley looking down at the sack enshrouded cat.

'Is it alive?' I asked, not detecting any movement in the sacking.

'Oh, I think so.' As if in answer the cat twitched in the region of where we presumed the head was situated. 'I felt it better to leave it in the sack for the vet.'

Unfortunately John Deer, the only one in the local veterinary practice who had some knowledge of the Kellas cats, was away but another vet agreed to see the animal. I was not at all sure he understood what he was being asked to handle so I felt Brian had acted sensibly in leaving the terrified animal sacked, even if we still had no idea of just how badly injured the poor creature was, or indeed if it was a Kellas cat we were dealing with.

The vet was waiting for his unusual emergency and took the sacking bundle from us to the inner sanctum of the surgery, refusing to allow me to be present when it was sedated and unsacked on the grounds of public health and safety. The reasoning behind this rule was somewhat obscure as I had been present when animals have had to be put down and have actually been asked to hold the animals during the injection. I'd also attended a post-mortem on a dead lamb in the same veterinary practice. Another vet arrived and asked me if I wanted to look at the cat once it was out. I agreed gratefully. After all, if the unfortunate animal was badly injured and was not a Kellas but a feral cat, it would be more sensible to put it to sleep rather than attempting to save it.

I walked into the room and looked at the unconscious animal stretched out on the table for the first time.

'It's a big cat,' said the vet.

It was. It was also a Kellas.

'I'm afraid the leg will have to come off. That paw is a real mess.' He lifted the swollen mangled front paw which was badly crushed, presumably by the descending door of the trap, or else it was trapped between wires of the mesh in the animal's struggle to escape. If the latter, then I felt the past battle to acquire the spot welded mesh had been more than worth the trouble.

'How will it manage without a leg?' I asked. 'Will it be able to adapt?' Desperate as I was to save the life of the Kellas, I didn't want to be cruel and cause it unnecessary suffering.

'No problem,' said the vet cheerfully. 'A cat will cope with the loss of a leg easily without it really affecting its lifestyle. Although it's only the paw that is injured, it's better to remove the whole leg, it avoids complications afterwards.'

I nodded and turned to leave, then I suddenly remembered. 'What sex is it?' I asked.

'Female,' the vet said.

If it survived the shock and the operation, we had another mate for Fred.

'Will it be able to mate and breed with a limb missing?'

'Oh yes,' said the vet, lifting up the limp body to take it away for surgery.

I went home to worry about what I was going to do with the cat when it recovered from its operation. In its weakened state, I couldn't put it into the enclosure with the others. They would almost certainly attack and kill it. Brian had agreed to loan me his cage for the weekend, but he needed it back urgently in case he had a call for an injured seal; it was the only cage he had that was suitable for the purpose. The Kellas was too large to keep in a normal metal mesh cat basket and once she recovered from the anesthetic she was going to be in a fury and able to do considerable damage, even with three legs and missing front teeth!

An hour later I was back at the vet's to collect the still unconscious cat only to find that there was no way I could get the cage into my car. We struggled for a few minutes, then tried the boot, but whichever way you looked at it, the cage was too large or the car too small.

Gasping with the exertion, we plonked the huge box with the soundly sleeping cat on the pavement.

'It's no good,' I sighed. 'There's no way to fit it in. How long will she be out?'

'Oh, she'll asleep for about another hour,' said the vet.

I suggested we laid the cat on the back seat and tied the box to the back of the car as the journey would only take fifteen minutes at the most, even driving slowly. Once home I could untie the box and put the cat back in, still giving me a half hour before she began to recover. It was not ideal but it seemed the only way.

The vet pressed me to use one of their baskets, rather than leave the cat lying on the back seat and I agreed. Luckily . . .

Within a minute of pulling away, I heard a lunging movement from the basket. The cat was not aware it had another hour of sleep and it was coming to! I put my foot down to get home at speed, I did not fancy transferring a rampaging Kellas that had just discovered she'd lost her freedom, her teeth and a leg all in the same day. When I opened the vet's basket and put my hand in, I wanted to do it when the basket contained a still doped patient.

It was a short drive but the Kellas was a fast waker. By the time I pulled up at the door she was struggling to sit up and spitting furiously as she constantly toppled over. The cage was unstrapped from the back of the car at speed and we lugged it through the house into the freezer room, which was the only place I could think of to put it. Then I carried in the basket containing the dazed, bewildered but furious cat. With every second she was becoming more aware of her surroundings and I had to get her out of the basket quick, I didn't even have a pair of leather gauntlets for protection. I took my courage literally into my hands and, opening the basket, thrust my arm in and grabbed the struggling cat by the scruff of the neck. Fortunately, although she was now wide awake, her legs – those she had left – were still weak and not responding to her movements. Seconds later she was safely back in the box and I still had all my fingers. I slammed the front lock in place and stood back. I was shaking with relief.

The poor cat twisted and turned, trying to rise and unable to understand why she kept toppling forward on her injured shoulder. Her eyes blazed at me and she spat and hissed her confusion and terror. Instead of standing, her remaining legs sprawled beneath her weight and she clawed the floor with her remaining front leg, dragging herself around in tight circles. I threw a heavy blanket over the box to shut out the light and keep her warm, then I left her in peace to sleep away the effects of the anesthetic.

I checked the cat at intervals throughout the night. She lay slumped in a drousy heap, pressed against the back of the cage, but her eyes were bright and alert and she stared at me suspiciously. Her shoulder where the limb had been amputated was shaven to the grey skin but the wound was hardly visible. No bleeding or swollen area was apparent.

The next morning she was a little more active when disturbed, spitting angrily and trying to strike at me in the enclosed space, rising up on her one good front leg and attempting to lunge forward, only to topple over on to her injured shoulder. She did not seem to understand what had been done to her and was unable to comprehend that she no longer had two good front legs to balance a frontal attack. Distressing as it was to see her pain and confusion, I was glad to witness her continued hostility as it suggested she was

not sinking into shocked lethargy. That is the real killer of
injured animals.

Yet, if she was going to survive the operation, I had another
problem to solve, and swiftly. Over the weekend I had to
construct a second enclosure suitable for a three-legged
Kellas. I decided to use the inner L-shaped side of the existing
Kellas pen, giving me only two sides and a roof to build. As
well as needing less materials, using the existing structure
would also enable her to see and smell the other two cats,
and that might help her to accept captivity. It would also give
me a chance to gauge the reaction of the others to her. Eventually mating her with Fred was my cherished aim.

Although the new enclosure was much smaller than the
main one, it was nevertheless a dawn to dusk construction
job. Luckily I had posts, wood and some wire left over from
the first enclosure and so, armed with a hammer, three
pounds of large nails, a couple of pounds of staples and a
couple of helpers, I set to work.

I decided that I did not need to dig down into the
foundations, as the army had done, in order to bury the wire
in concrete for, despite our carefully considered precautions,
the two cats had never shown any inclination to dig their way
out, and it seemed highly unlikely that a three legged cat
could dig anyway. Instead I planked the bottom of the run, so
providing a draught-proof base. For a sleeping den I decided
to copy the chest of drawers conversion that had been so
successful in the main enclosure. The only difficulty was that
I hadn't got another old unwanted chest of drawers and I
hadn't time to try and scrounge one. Ah, well, needs must!

I emptied the old pine chest of drawers in my bedroom,
tossing the contents in a pile on the floor and dragging the
large chest through the house to the garden. It seemed
sacrilege to destroy a perfectly good Victorian chest but the
cat had to be rehoused swiftly to allow her to adjust to her
new conditions and Brian could at any time need his box back
for an injured seal, or fox, or badger. I spent the weekend
frantically sawing, hammering and stapling with a will, and

by six o'clock on the Sunday night had it finished. The sleeping den was stuffed with straw and a small step built to assist a three-legged cat to enter her sleeping quarters. I was bruised, battered, aching and knackered.

The task had been made more difficult because of the constant attentions of Fred, who had spent the entire time pacing up and down the wire that separated the two enclosures, just waiting for any opportunity to lash out through the mesh at unprotected bodies momentarily forgetting his presence. When he couldn't reach legs or arms by striking through the wire, he would sink down, watching patiently until he was certain he had been forgotten, and then at a crucial moment, usually with perfect timing just as one was about to bring down the hammer, he would launch himself at the mesh, throwing himself at it with a crash and a loud furious *Phaah*! The results of these attacks were me leaping about holding blackening fingers and cursing loudly.

As the light was fading on the Sunday night the new run was complete and ready for its three-legged occupant. We hauled the box containing the growling cat out to the enclosure and sliding up the run door and securing it, we pinned the box against the entrance. Then it was only a case of opening the box's sliding door and leaving the cat to gather the courage to venture out into her new home. It could take all night, at best a couple of hours, before she would risk leaving the shelter of the dark box to stagger out into the open. Because of her injury, I had to let her take her own time. We couldn't shake the box to help dislodge her as we had with the other two cats. She had not yet had the opportunity to try walking on three legs and it would take time for her to learn to balance with a missing limb.

So I thought.

As I pulled the sliding door towards me, there was a sudden flash of black across the run and she was gone, only the tip of her tail visible in the narrow gap under the sleeping den. Then even that vanished.

I was dismayed that she had not found the entrance to her

sleeping quarters and worried that squashing herself into such a tiny space beneath it could have torn her stitches and reopened the wound, but there was nothing I could do. I tossed a rabbit into the run and secured the catch of the gate. Fred hung on the wire and tried to reach the rabbit, eyes gleaming with anticipation.

'Sorry lad, it's not yours.'

I opened the outer door of the main enclosure and went in carrying two more rabbits. I unlatched his door and was about to toss the first rabbit into the enclosure when there was a sudden whirlwind of black fur and it was wrenched from my hand. Fred wasn't waiting, he was taking! With satisfied growls, he straddled the rabbit and, glaring at me, daring me to retrieve it, stalked off stiff-legged towards the hut.

For weeks I had been trying to gain enough courage to persuade him to take the food from my hand and then it had happened by accident. I tossed in the second rabbit to Freda and closed the door. It was finished. The new cat would either live or die; I had done all I could.

I was so shattered I could hardly lift my arms to drink a cup of coffee. My muscles were taut and strained, I wasn't sure I hadn't fractured a finger, and I was black and blue with bruises. That night I was too tired to sleep.

The next morning I limped out at dawn to see if the new cat was still squashed under the sleeping den or whether she had managed to find her way into the chest. Unfortunately she was still underneath but I could tell she was alive. A ridge of black back bulged out at the rear and this heaved slightly with rhythmic breathing. Her food was untouched, much to Fred's disappointment. He clung to the wire mesh, his paws thrust through, desperately trying to reach the rejected rabbit. He gazed at me with huge golden eyes. 'I can't get it,' he seemed to be begging. 'Can you pass it to me?'

I'd never seen him look so cute. It was amazing what a bit of desperate pleading could do.

There was no sign of Freda; clearly the disruption of the

past two days had destroyed her recently found courage and she had again retreated to the dark safety of her sleeping den.

That evening Fred was still positioned hanging through the mesh, trying to hook his neighbour's rabbit. He collected his own supper but one had the feeling the night would be spent fishing through the wire after the coveted bunny.

Next morning I was amazed to see the rabbit had been shifted slightly, though whether this was by Fred's contortions or by the rabbit's legitimate owner I had no way of knowing. Fred was still hanging through the bars, and I decided he might as well have it as the new cat did not seem to be ready for food. She had been out during the night for I could see a latrine area in the straw. Although minus a leg, she had not achieved the tidy heap that was her neighbours' trade mark. As I hauled out the rabbit Fred looked horrified. I'd nicked his rabbit! When he saw me heading towards his door, he leapt across and stood on his hind legs to peer out of the meshed upper part of the door, his eyes huge golden orbs, his ears pricked appealingly, his large velvet paws groping through the wire desperately pleading. For the first time, I could see no malice or hatred in his beautiful eyes. He was really asking me, not demanding or ordering, but asking! I could not see his rear but I had visions of his tail wagging like an eager puppy dog.

I opened the door cautiously and stepped into the enclosure, holding the rabbit out. Fred rushed forward and grabbed it but this time I was ready for him and held on. I let him tug it, then pulled it back towards me in a tug of war. Then I let go and he sprang away. I was delighted with him. I had finally persuaded him to accept food from me, I had hand fed a Kellas.

For the next two days the new cat used her toilet area and found her way into the sleeping den where she nestled down out of sight in the straw. I had no way of knowing whether her wound was healing or how I could get any more antibiotics into her if there was any infection. She was still showing no interest in food.

Uneasy Truce

At feeding time on the third day Fred and Freda were both outside, waiting for me. Freda had regained her courage to face me in the open. She spat and growled, her small nose wrinkling, her whiskers quivering as she approached the mesh and made no attempt to race for cover. Only the new cat was keeping its distance, but with the other two feeding within sight of it, I was hopeful that it would gain courage from their behaviour and begin to feed when it felt up to it.

10

Matters of Life and Death

The new Kellas had been six days without food and I was begining to get seriously worried. Cats frequently fast for short periods but, in her weakened state, not eating could only make her recovery from surgery more difficult. I tried chopped and minced meat and even liver, but every morning the juicy titbits remained untouched, to be lusted over by dribbling Fred. There was no need for him to panic; he and Freda acquired the extras every morning, still edible if a bit past their sell-by date.

One night I heard a low rumbling call coming from the cat pen. I stood in the darkness in the garden and listened. It was Fred pacing up and down his enclosure, wailing softly in a low musical tone. The wailing bore no resemblance to the high-pitched sound made by a domestic tom; it was a quiet, almost conversational sound, very deep and guttural. As soon as I moved to approach the pen, the sound ceased immediately.

Freda regained her courage quickly. Every feeding time she was lined up at the wire waiting for her supper, despite experiencing a few vicious swipes from her companion. It was the first opportunity I'd had to see them together and they certainly were not an ideal couple. They showed no affection towards each other, unlike domestic cats that frequently indulge in mutual grooming sessions and greet each other by brushing the scent glands on their faces together with a kissing motion and rubbing their bodies against one another, weaving around in a complicated movement in the same way as they rub against their human companion's legs. The best one could say about Freddy and Freda was they tolerated each other and shared the sleeping den without constant aggression towards each other. There was no sign of friendship between them. It was as if they had been imprisoned together and were making the best of it.

Freda also began to spend more time out of her sleeping den, sitting in the centre of the pen, watching me feed the other animals. She was small, half the size of Fred, with a very delicate pointed face, her head tiny compared to her overall body length which was long and slender with a bushy wildcat tail.

Like Fred, she was jet black with a small white star on her chest, the light patch just visible on her underbelly, and her flanks and hind quarters were liberally sprinkled with the long white guard hairs so typical of the Kellas cats. I was undecided if she was a diluted Kellas or just a very small one, but if her appearance was uncertain, her nature was not. If anything, she was even more vicious than her massive mate. Her big golden eyes glared hatred, her lips were pulled back in an almost permanent snarl, her sharp white teeth highlighted against the bright red of her curling tongue. Her height was difficult to judge as she never seemed to move in anything other than a crouched position or belly crawl, though whether this was due to Fred's constant attacks or fear of me, I was unable to determine. Her slinking posture made her look boney with jutting hips and shoulder blades.

If Freda was willing to be viewed, the new cat was certainly not. There was no sound or sight of the sulking three-legged newcomer during the day, although I was certain she was alive because every morning the straw on the floor of her pen had been scrabbled through and rearranged. After a week without eating she still was making no attempt to take the food left for her. I lay awake at night, praying that she would accept that evening's offerings, having visions of her huddled in her sleeping den, buried in the straw, frightened, in pain and slowly starving to death.

Yet the daily evidence suggested that, far from cowering in the sleeping den, she had been extremely active each night. Her toilet straw was alternatively heaped and scattered, dragged from one end of the pen to the other, and I began to notice what appeared to be scrape marks in the soil along the length of the wire dividing her enclosure from the other two cats. At first I thought it must be my imagination, that the soft soil had been turned over when the foundations were dug out and I hadn't noticed it before. Neither Fred nor Freda had ever tried to dig out of their enclosure and they had four good legs apiece. Surely if four-legged cats had not attempted to tunnel their escape, a three-legged one would not have burrowing ambitions. As the soil became more furrowed, I still would not accept the evidence.

On the eleventh morning, however, there was a surprising development. The meat was still untouched but I could no longer ignore the diggings. A hole about a foot deep had appeared at the base of one of the posts, exposing the buried concrete. She might not be eating, but the new cat certainly didn't seem to be weakening, despite her lack of sustenance. I looked at the hole, amazed. How could a starving animal with only one front leg dig at all, never mind tackle the hard-packed stoney ground where we had buried the posts and wire? How long could she keep up her strength without eating? I consulted the vet and went through the menu that had already been rejected.

The vet shrugged. 'All I can think of is to try live food,' he suggested.

He was putting words to my own thoughts, but I just couldn't do it. I couldn't leave a terrified living animal in the pen to await a predator's attack. Yet, with only three Kellas cats in captivity, could I leave one of them to starve to death just because I was squeamish?

I looked at my unwanted cockerel. He cocked his head appealingly and gazed back trustingly out of bright boot-button eyes. I remembered him as a fluffy little chick, living in a box in my bedroom, chirping eagerly for his human fostermother to provide the chick with crumbs after his real mother had successfully hatched out him and his sisters on a neighbouring farm and then promptly keeled over and died. The orphan chicks had been found by the farmer, huddled under the dead body and within hours they were tucked up in a box in my bedroom under a lamp to keep them warm. I didn't want a cockerel, but could I betray my foster son by feeding him to the starving cat?

No. I should, but I couldn't do it.

I thought of a possible compromise. The pathetic blind rabbits with myxomatosis that could be seen huddled on roadside verges, terrified, waiting for death to release them from their misery. Although I cannot normally kill, these rabbits are the exception to my rule. On spotting one, I always stop the car, catch it and dispatch it swiftly with a quick chop to the back of the neck. Such a rabbit, blinded and weakened, would not be aware of its surroundings and the danger it was in and would provide an easy-to-kill live prey for a cat – even one with a missing leg and no front teeth!.

I didn't like the idea but neither did I like the thought of the poor cat having survived trapping, amputation and captivity, finally dying of starvation. The one obstacle was that I didn't have a rabbit dying of myxomatosis. The vet promised to provide me with any that came his way, but would we get one before the cat died of starvation?

On the morning of the twelfth day I went out to inspect the run for any night-time activity. This daily inspection was the only means I had of assessing whether the new cat was still alive or had died in the night. If there were no visible signs for four or five days, then the vet and I felt it would be a reasonable risk to poke inside the den for any reaction. However, the idea of thrusting one's hand into the straw containing a still living Kellas was a daunting one, even if the cat had missing teeth and was minus a clawed paw.

Fred as usual was waiting for me and flew at the wire with a flurry of straw and earth as he lashed out and tore at the ground in a token act of aggression, then, honour satisfied, he sank down and watched me lazily, licking his lips in anticipation, waiting for his morning titbits rejected by his new neighbour.

For once he was to be disappointed. The new cat's dish was empty, chunks of beef and pork and slices of ox liver, all were gone! Twelve days after capture she had decided to accept her new conditions and the food offered. There now seemed no obstacle to her survival. For the first time since her capture, I began to believe I had another potential mate for Fred.

I considered carefully at what stage I should risk them meeting and whether I should give the new cat access to the other cats' enclosure, or else put Fred in the new cat's smaller pen.

It would be safer to make a small entrance from the new pen into the old, allowing the new female access to and from while preventing the bulkier tom from following her to the safety of her own quarters. If Fred had lived alone, this would be the obvious choice, but Fred did not live alone; Freda lived with him, and although she was smaller than the other two cats, she had the advantage of two front legs if matched against the new cat. Her size also meant that whatever opening could be constructed for the new cat to use, Freda would use it as well. This could result in Freda stealing the new cat's food before she had ventured out to collect it, and if Freda did take objection to Fred's second mate, the disabled cat would have nowhere to seek sanctuary from Freda's aggression.

The alternative solution, of putting Fred into the new cat's enclosure, posed different problems. If the meeting did not go well, she would have nowhere to escape the heavier ferocious tom who would more than likely kill her. Also there were the practicalities of separating Fred and Freda in order to get Fred alone into the new cat's enclosure.

It was a difficult decision to make. The wrong move could result in disaster, with dead or seriously injured cats to retrieve from the enclosure. I only had to watch the displays of aggression between Fred and Freda, who had been together for four years, to be conscious of the serious risks involved in introducing the three cats to each other. Yet if I did not take the risk, the two female Kellas cats could not breed, and that defeated the whole idea of keeping them in captivity.

In addition, I was still left with the old problem of how to separate Freda from Fred if there was any sign of her being pregnant. We knew she had kitted in the autumn of the previous year because of a single sighting of a kitten by a keeper at the Highland Wildlife Park but whether she herself had killed and eaten the litter because of the proximity of the male was impossible to judge. What did appear obvious was that if Freda herself hadn't killed them, Fred almost certainly would have done it. I also wondered whether there had been other litters, unknown to the park staff, that had met the same fate. It seemed highly likely.

If the Highland Wildlife Park had given us time to complete the internal structure of the pen, it would have been a fairly simple task to lure the cats apart by separate feeding areas and lock the dividing partition to prevent them getting back together. Now, with Fred constantly on the alert and ready for instant attack, the problem was how to get inside the enclosure and work on a method of dividing the pen up in safety.

And Fred was not giving an inch. It was either a very brave or a very foolhardy intruder who would dare to take on Fred on his own territory, not to mention the complication of a newly couragous Freda bringing up a rear attack. There was no way of spending any time working within the enclosure without drugging the protective pair unconcious. But I had to do something. If we couldn't work on the inside, then it had to be done on the outside.

I still had a fractured finger from building the extension

for the new cat, but it looked as if extension two was about to go on the drawing board. If I could make another small pen for Freda, with her own sleeping quarters away from Fred, it would serve a dual purpose. It would be somewhere to put her if she showed signs of pregnancy. With the kittens in her own enclosure, Fred couldn't get at them. It might also be possible to construct it in such a way that I could gain access to the kittens without Freda's knowledge. I had hand-reared domestic kittens in the past and was convinced that it would be possible to rear a semi-tame Kellas if only one could get a kitten away from the mother. If the sleeping den had a rear hatch it might be possible to fish out a kitten while Freda was out of the den getting her own supper without her even being aware one was missing. Dividing the litter would also give at least one kitten a chance to survive if it had been Freda and not Fred that had killed the kittens born in the park.

The planned new extension would have a secondary purpose. Once Freda was securely away from Fred, it would lessen the problems of introducing the new cat to him, for if she were in season, it was unlikely that he would not accept her and she would be able to enter and leave his enclosure at will, without him having access to her pen through the smaller opening. The difficulty with the plan was to construct an entrance between the main enclosure and the two smaller pens that would be too small to allow Fred to squeeze through but be large enough to allow easy passage for the female cats. Despite his bulk, Fred was pretty adept at squashing into small spaces, which he'd proved by immediately taking over the sleeping den intended for Freda alone.

If I got my calculations wrong this time, the results could be the end of the Kellas breeding plans. It could also be the end of one of the female Kellases. And I couldn't exactly measure Fred when designing the entrance holes.

While I was puzzling and planning, the new cat was attempting to take matters into her own three paws by nightly tunnelling in the direction of Fred and Freda's homeland, though whether her motives were friendship, lust or aggression it was impossible to guess. All one could say was that she seemed determined to reach the second enclosure rather that dig her way out in a simple escape bid. There was no evidence of her ever having a swift scratch at the outer mesh, which was just as well since I had not been able to sink the wire in concrete like Gary had. My construction, although not flimsy, certainly lacked depth, but then I had not anticipated that a cat missing one front leg would have either the ability or the inclination to join the Miners' Union.

Every morning I studied the new furrows and fresh holes and wondered how she managed to achieve such results. Then I noticed signs of a different and equally amazing activity. The wooden chest of drawers that had been converted to her sleeping accommodation was showing distinct signs of wear. The wood around the entrance was being nibbled away as if by a giant rodent.

I looked around and found other areas of deeply chewed wood. But the new cat had lost her front teeth. I had examined the torn and bleeding gums myself when she'd been stretched out unconscious on the vet's table. How could she be chewing her way through house and home?

A horrible thought struck me. Was the new cat still alive or had she died soon after her operation and something else taken over her sleeping den, possibly having devoured her mortal remains before starting on her evening meals? Now, not satisfied with the fast food delivery service, was it sharpening its fangs on the fabric of the actual hotel? It was an unsettling thought.

I frequently had glimpses of stoats and weasels, lithe reddish-brown long slender bodies dashing across paths and lanes in a continuous search for prey. The enclosure was only a few yards from the burn that I knew was frequented by mink and less glamorous but just as lethal rats. Any one of these carnivorous rodents could have squeezed themselves through the enclosure wire with ease, all would be more than happy to dispose of my nightly offerings of rabbit, pork and beef and all could be tunnelling under the wire or gnawing holes in the woodwork as a form of occupational therapy. The more I considered it, the more likely it seemed.

But how to find out?

Who or whatever their neighbour was, Fred and Freda seemed unperturbed, neither showing any interest in the occupant of the adjoining pen other than a frustrated lust for the nightly tasty portions dropped through the wire. Freda was now out every day, studying everyone or anything that passed with a bright golden icy stare. I wondered what their reaction would be to other animals, and I was to find out one morning when I discovered one of my neighbour's ewes staggering down the lane, presumably having escaped from her hillside field.

Stray hill sheep are a way of life in the country, but normally they would bound off at the slightest suggestion of an approach by strangers. The routine is to herd them back across the river where they normally find their way back through the wire with the same ease as they had escaped. In this case, however, the ewe stood quietly as I approached and allowed me to touch her. I thought she might be ill. I led her into my field but she was promptly bowled over in the rush of my own animals to investigate. I heaved the ewe up on her feet but within minutes she had collapsed again. I half-dragged and half-carried her to the small paddock where the cat's enclosure was situated. I made up a rough shelter for her, gave her straw, hay, feed and water, and was rewarded by a grateful nuzzle and a weary bleat. Then I phoned the farmer.

By the time he had arrived the ewe was settled in and grazing happily, although still tottery on her legs.

'She's just old,' he said. 'I've a few of them at the moment. With the poor prices last year, it wasn't worth selling them off, so I just kept them with the flock to let nature take its course. She's due to lamb in a few weeks and I guess it's just taken it out of her.'

The ewe watched us, as contentedly she chewed cud.

'Leave her with me,' I said. 'If you put her back on the hill she won't have a chance, I don't mind looking after her, to see if we can keep her going until she's lambed.'

The farmer nodded. 'Well, if you don't mind, she'll have a better chance as you'll have more time for her. If she dies, I'll come up and take away the carcase.'

By now the ewe and I had become firm friends. She grazed happily around the cats' enclosure without any apparent reaction from Fred or Freda, although I was still subjected to murderous attacks on sight. When I stood at the enclosure talking to them, or at feeding times, the old ewe would toddle over and stand companionably by my side like a dog, staring at the cats with obvious interest. Then one morning, as Fred threw himself at the wire, the ewe bent her head and to my amazement the two animals sniffed each other, their noses almost touching through the wire. I froze, expecting the ewe to suffer a slashed nose from Fred's razor claws, but nothing happened. They snuffled and snorted in a friendly way until the ewe, satisfied with the introduction, lifted her head and nuzzled my hand. Fred, his eyes glowing with a softened look, suddenly remembered where he was, where I was, and with a growl threw himself at the wire with a screaming *Phaaah*!

He might be at peace with sheep but humans were a different proposition.

The old ewe settled happily into her new home but age had taken its toll and one day she collapsed, her legs just folding under her, no longer able to take her weight. The farmer shook his head sadly.

'Nothing to be done, I'm afraid,' he said. 'None of us can fight age. The old girl's just come to the end of her time.'

I helped her over to her shelter and supported her body with a straw bank so that she couldn't roll over on her back. She settled down comfortably though she refused to eat and I knew it was just a matter of time. I checked her every hour or so and was always greeted with a gentle bleat of welcome as she lifted her head tiredly to give my face a soft nuzzle before closing her eyes and sinking back into a deep sleep. That night she slipped quietly away, no panic, no thrashing about. She simply died in her sleep.

I was sad we couldn't save the lambs but I was glad to have shared the old ewe's life at the end and happy that she had at least experienced the comfort of a pet's life for just a little while. The cats watched the farmer take away her body. I wondered if Fred's behaviour towards her had been one of conscious friendship. His passive eyes said nothing as he watched the old ewe being dragged away.

11

Playing Lamb and Cat

A few days after the death of the ewe, the spring weather was a thing of the past and winter finally arrived, late but eager. Within hours the weather had changed from mild, with budding daffodils and pools of nodding snowdrops along the river bank, to harsh blizzard conditions, the vicious wind cutting an icy swathe across the valleys, heaping drifts of snow across the roads, cutting off all routes in and out of the mountains. The skiers celebrated but the farmers shook their heads miserably and bitterly muttered 'Lambing storms'.

Luckily most of the ewes were still off the hills despite the mild winter and they huddled in groups on the lower slopes, sheltering from the harsh snow-laden winds against the slight protection of fences and hedges, small snow-covered humps just detectable in the fields as they waited out the storm, looking like giant snowballs. My Hebridean flock looked worse than the local commercial breeds of Suffolk and Cheviot because, being black with long fine straight coats, the snow stood out on their fleece, the spikey ends forming tiny icicles and icy crusts. My pet Suffolk, Piddles, who was heavily pregnant, lumbered through the snow looking pathetically miserable and I had to take the two Clydesdales up to a neighbouring farm to shelter for the duration of the blizzard.

Although the late snow made life difficult for every living thing except the operators of the ski resorts, who were facing bankruptcy, and the holidaymakers who used them, it did have one advantage for me. The new cat's pen revealed prints showing where the occupant had paced and delved around when dining out. And they were cat prints.

The mystery was solved. The new cat was alive and well. Her health was suggested by tracks in the snow on top of her sleeping den where she had prowled and sat, the scuff marks and prints like a diary of her night's activities. It was obvious that she had completely adjusted to the loss of her leg and was able to leap up on to the four-foot-high shelf with complete ease.

The sudden storms passed as swiftly as they had come. Within days the roads were cleared and the fields were showing green grass. The sheep shook their woollen backs to dislodge the last lumps of ice caught in their fleeces and went back to the serious business of eating and lambing.

Piddles was due on the Tuesday, and as it was her first time and she had been bottle-reared from a day old, neither of us were quite sure how we would manage.

'Bottle-reared lambs,' muttered farmers gloomily, 'never amount to anything.' Piddles was built like a small Chieftan tank.

'Ewes that are too fat don't become fertile,' was another general piece of advice. Piddles was definitely fat and appeared to be getting fatter. I hoped it was a sign of fertility rather than a need for starvation.

'If they do take, fat ewes and first timers usually only have single births.'

That I felt was just as well as it was my first experience at lambing, as well as Piddles'.

The final pearl of wisdom thrown at me was: 'Bottle-feds make bad mothers. They just don't know what to do with the lambs, and often as not will walk off and leave them to die.'

If Piddles did that, I would be there with at least my proven bottle-rearing ability.

The dates said Tuesday, Piddles said otherwise. I planned to bring her up to the cats' paddock on the Sunday before. At six o'clock on the Friday morning I noticed Piddles seated in the field shelter that no one ever used. At six thirty I was meeting her healthy and loved twin sons, one white with black splodges, the other black with diffused white patches.

Well, Piddles never had been good at dates, or at listening to expert advice.

The sudden thaw had resulted in thick mud churned to a clammy morass, especially around the shelter where the horses had ploughed up the mire to a depth of feet. Piddles sat in isolated splendour on dry straw in the shelter, the roof being too low to admit the horses. Surrounded as she was by the boggy mess, I had visions of her new wobbly-legged lambs being swallowed up without trace the moment they ventured out into the big world. I decided that moving them was the first urgent act of the day. I picked up the still wet, slightly bloody bleating babies and, with Piddles trailing behind, I led the way down the lane to the garden. The new mother was delighted with her change of accommodation, her ambition having always been to return to the garden following her youthful ban. Now, instead of sneaking in, she was being invited in. Piddles' cup of happiness was overflowing. I even ignored her first defiant grab at my poor long-suffering roses.

Although she had the freedom of the garden for the first day, she had to be contained for her own safety and that of her tiny twins in case they wandered on to the road. In the evening she was led to her old nursery paddock at the side of the house where she had been kept during her bottle-fed days. It was home sweet home for Piddles – except for the new structure in the centre. She wandered up and examined the cats' enclosure, staring at Fred who sat eyeing her in turn.

I wondered if she would receive the same companionable treatment as the old ewe. Certainly neither Fred nor Freda seemed at all put out on seeing her. I supposed it was nature's way. Both cats would have encountered sheep in the wild, and as the cats were not big enough to prey on sheep and the sheep in turn had no aggressive interest in the cats, there was no reason in the world why they could not live side by side as good neighbours.

The two little lambs were a different proposition however. Newborn weak lambs would be suitable natural prey to the cats, but I hoped that the combination of Piddles guarding her new offspring, the existence of the wire, and the fact that the cats were fed regularly and so could not be hungry, would give them enough protection if they strayed too close to the mesh.

As an added precaution I put some length of wood along the base of the outside of the enclosure in the hope it would prevent the lambs getting within reach of Fred's strike.

Of course, as is usual when dealing with animals, they immediately do the very thing you are trying to avoid. Within five minutes of being in the paddock, the black lamb staggered across to the new cat's wire and collapsed against it to snuggle up for a snooze. Fred studied the tiny figure intently though it was well out of his reach. Oblivious of her young son's danger, Piddles munched happily, her black nose rooting through the tangled grass.

I sighed and gave up. It was time for my breakfast.

I checked on the lambs throughout the day, wanting to be certain that Piddles was feeding both successfully and had enough milk. I need not have worried; her own milk might have come out of a bottle, but her babies were not deprived of natural resources.

That night Fred and Freda were lined up waiting for their supper, snarling and hissing as usual. They watched me feed the other animals, standing on their hind legs and peering through the wire, their necks stretched, their ears pricked, red tongues licking their lips in anticipation.

The lambs were curled up asleep in the straw of the sheep shelter, warm, dry and safe. It had been a long and tiring day. Piddles was lying proudly beside them, contently chewing cud though she quickly hauled her still massive bulk to her feet at the sight of the feed bag.

The slight delay feeding Piddles before reaching the cats meant that I was subjected to a torrent of abuse when finally I arrived with the meat pail. As I dropped the strips in they were snatched from my hand in a flurry of fur and spitting fury, Fred dashing for the shed and Freda heading in a blur for the den. I had the feeling the cats were not amused at being last in the supper queue.

I checked the lambs by torchlight during the night but all was peaceful, the lambs curled up sleeping, mum dozing, and Fred quietly pacing around his run, his eyes glowing greeny yellow as he turned startled to face the torch beam. I had hoped to catch a glimpse of the new cat but I was unlucky; her run was empty.

The following day I relaxed a little, though still feared the sight of a mangled lamb dragged to the mesh. But the cats seemed disinterested in their new neighbours and the lambs were more concerned with keeping an eye on their trundling milkbar mum and finding out how to keep control of their long legs.

They were a cute combination, the Hebridian Suffolk cross more like kids than lambs, with fine featured goat-like heads sporting tiny well developed horn buds, slender long-legged build and large eyes. Their baby coats were soft and fluffy, unlike the tight coarse wool of Suffolk lambs, and they were completely contrasting in colour.

On the third day I robbed Piddles of her babies for an hour while I took them over to Lynn for her husband to ring them to castrate and dock their tails. This was a painless operation at their young age. Rubber bands were slipped around the testicles and halfway down the tail, cutting off the blood supply and eventually causing the unwanted bits to drop off. The lambs were fine, though poor Piddles had roared the place down while searching for her lost youngsters, having been diverted by buns while I did the evil deed.

On my return I found her glaring suspiciously at an innocent looking Fred who was sitting unconcernedly on the roof of his den, calmly licking his chops.

The joy of mother when she found that her babies had not provided Fred and Freda with a light afternoon snack was touching, leaving me with a very guilty feeling as I walked in carrying the lambs with a cheery 'Do these belong to you, Pids? You ought to keep an eye on them!'

That evening at feeding time Fred did his usual post-climbing act as I reached the mesh, his feet, wicked claws extended, reaching through the wire on either side of the post, his broad snarling face almost level with mine, Freda crouched below him, growling viciously, her tail fluffed out like a squirrel's, lashing from side to side, her teeth gleaming white against her red mouth. I produced the first glistening chunk of meat and Fred dropped down in anticipation, positively drooling. However he wasted valuable moments making a last lunge at me and Freda saw her chance. She whipped in under his striking paw and hooked the meat from right under his nose, turning tail with it and fleeing with the speed of an express train to the safety of her den.

Fred dropped down, amazed. The meat was gone! He glared at me '*Phaah!*' It had to be my fault. I dropped in the next chunk and he grabbed it without further macho display and headed for his shelf in the shed. Freda's face appeared grinning in the entrance to her den. She could never have eaten it so swiftly; she must have secreted it in a safe place. I dropped the next two chunks through the wire and then moved round to the new cat's compound. I dropped the meat through on to the platform in front of her sleeping den and then, as usual, peered into the darkness through the entrance hole. A pair of golden eyes gazed back, unblinking. There was no sound, no movement, and I could see nothing of her body shape in the dim light, but she was studying me intently, just as Freda had done before gaining enough courage to appear in daylight. I crouched down and looked at her. The new cat did not flinch or sink down in the straw; she just stared back, no expression other than curiosity in her shining eyes. I talked softly to her, just as I had at first to Fred and Freda, speaking any nonsense simply to get her used to the sound of my voice. Then I straightened up and walked quietly away, not wishing to push that first fleeting contact too far too fast.

As I looked back Fred dashed out to retrieve the last piece of meat, pausing to look at me with the beef clutched in his teeth. I remembered how he used to flee at the sight of me. Would the new cat soon be climbing the wire to grab its supper?

I felt for the first time that she should have a name and what better than Kelly, after the estate where she had been caught.

Piddles' head butted me to check for tit bits, her black nose delving into my pocket on a bun hunt. Motherhood had not altered her behaviour or her greed. The two lambs gambolled up to me, pausing to stare, their long legs stuck out at all angles as they had not yet learnt how to coordinate their movements. I patted Piddles and went off to fill the watering can to top up her water trough. When I returned with the desired couple of buns and fresh water, Fred was back in the enclosure, pacing up and down. I was still on the other side of the fence when I saw the little white lamb rubbing his three-day-old horn buds against a tree and I watched fascinated as he carefully positioned the slender tree trunk against his forehead and nodded franticly, scratching the embryonic horns against the rough bark. Then he bounced off towards the cat pen where Fred was pacing.

To my horror, the tiny lamb trotted up to the wire and pressed his horns against the mesh. There was nothing I could do except watch helplessly from the other side of the wooden fence. Fred stopped, turned and walked up to the tiny figure. Before my horrified eyes he reached the lamb as it was still pressed against the wire, in easy reach of those lashing paws.

Astonished, I watched Fred and the lamb gently sniff noses through the wire, actually touching. Then the lamb bounced off to see how the milk bar was doing and Fred returned to pacing his territory. I filled the ewe's trough thoughtfully.

It seemed that the cats' aggression was purely against man.

Even a helpless and doubtlessly prey-size lamb did not receive anything other than a friendly greeting. I had no doubt that if Fred had been hungry, the friendship might have been on rather insecure foundations, but obviously a well fed Fred had no evil intentions to anyone but his hereditary enemy.

As if to confirm my suspicions, he spotted me and spat. *'Phaah!'*

12

Developing Trust

Fred and Freda spent the wintry spring patrolling their enclosure or sitting on top of their den, regardless of the weather. Only very heavy rain drove them into the shelter of the shed; even fairly heavy snow didn't seem to deter them in any way, the snow flakes settling on their black fur and clinging to their whiskers in frosted icicles. Having accepted food from my hand, they now seldom bothered to wait for the bloody chunks to be dropped through the wire into their pen. Instead they launched themselves at the mesh as soon as I arrived, clawed paws reaching through the mesh long before the meat was within grasp.

Freda was asserting her authority more and more, frequently leaping in to snatch the largest chunk from directly under Fred's nose and rising up on her hind legs to strike at the unsuspecting tom without any apparent provocation on his part. He always struck back when attacked but never followed up, despite his larger build and superior strength. It was as if the power game had become reversed, and I wondered if the change in their behaviour towards one another was a prelude to mating. It was as if Freda were constantly keeping her male companion in check, whereas before she had been cowed by him, feeding only after he had finished and always relinquishing her position on the sleeping shelf if he required it. Now Fred seemed to have mellowed, even towards me, and he certainly no longer had the upper paw in the feline partnership. Freda on the other hand had become extremely aggressive, both towards me and her mate, spitting, lashing and snarling at both of us, a small bundle of constant fury.

Kelly continued to remain hidden, her missing food and the tunnelling activities the only sign of her existence. Yet, although she constantly attempted to burrow or chew her way through into the other cats' enclosure, there seemed to be no real interest on their part in the existence of their neighbour. The only attraction seemed to be the food when it was dropped into her pen and out of their reach. Then they would pace up and down, eyeing the apparently unwanted morsels until she had removed them, after which Fred and Freda lost interest.

Daily I hoped to see some sign of mating behaviour between the pair, but there was no hint of any change other than Freda's newly discovered courage and temper.

Piddles' lambs were growing at an alarming rate but the weather conditions were such that I did not feel it safe to return her to the muddy conditions in the field, fearing that the youngsters would become bogged down and drown, or die from exposure in the freezing wind. Had the cats shown any sign of striking at the lambs, I would have felt they were safer in the cold mud than within reach of grasping paws, but neither cat showed any inclination to attack the lambs. In fact, quite the opposite.

The lambs spent their time alternating between bouts of tremendous energy and short periods of total exhaustion when they slumped, dozing often against the cats' enclosure, their soft woolly backs pressed through the wire mesh. Fred and Freda would sometimes walk across and sniff the lambs but there was never any sign of aggression towards the outsiders.

Although Kelly was nowhere to be seen during the day, her nightly gnawing efforts were all too visible each morning.

She appeared to abandon her tunnelling and to concentrate on chewing her way to freedom. Two roof beams within reach of the top of her den were frayed and ripped, the frantic single-mindedness of her activities revealed one morning by spots of blood where she must have chewed at the rough wood until her mouth bled.

If the cats showed no interest in the reproductive joys of spring, the rest of the livestock made up for it. The geese decided that the icy winds of March were ideal for setting up house and nursery, two of them taking to the garden and hen house, much to the dismay of the hens which found themselves evicted from their own territory. To add to the confusion, the remainder of the geese in the field – worried about the missing homesteaders – set up a screeching dialogue between the two groups to reassure each other of their continued safe existence. One poor goose made her home in the clumps of rushes and sat out with great bravery the constant passing of rummaging sheep and clumping hooves the size of dinner plates as the Clydesdales lumbered past. The displacement of the hens by the geese gave me the added problem of discovering the hens' new laying places.

The Hebridean ewe and one ewe lamb showed definite swelling sides, but despite my constant hopes, each morning revealed the usual number of black grazing backs littering the field. With Piddles' proud achievement, my tup showed that he was fertile, and the ewes were healthy enough, so it was likely the tubby sides weren't just the result of too much feed. The tup continued to limp, his feet still bad, but any attempt to catch him was doomed to failure. He might have looked like a hobbling wreck when ambling around the field, but the moment a stranger appeared, he would become fleet-footed as any athlete with Olympic gold ambitions for the marathon and the high jump.

Twice a day I fed them and gradually the tup accepted my presence, as day by day, week by week, I gained his confidence. In the end I could actually stroke him without him flying off in a panic, even tickle his ears and rub his massive spread of curling horns, but such liberties were only tolerated if I was alone. And there lay the problem. I could catch him, but I hadn't the strength to hold him and trim his feet.

One day Wilson, from whom I'd bought my tiny flock, phoned me with a request. He needed to separate his new favourite young tup from the rest of his flock for a few weeks: could he run it and a ewe lamb with mine?

No problem.

In return he would be willing to take my tup away for a few weeks and treat his feet.

Now there was the problem!

First catch your tup, then treat it. Wilson and his shepherd, together with their two dogs, still had memories of the last time they had tried to catch my tup. We'd all ended up knackered, and the poor dogs were in a state of nervous collapse. Sheep were supposed to stand and quiver when cornered, not take flying leaps over the heads of hard working professional sheep dogs.

I decided stealth and cunning were the order of the day, and so, when Wilson and his shepherd arrived with his young tup and ewe, I organised an almost foolproof catching campaign. I left the two men hidden on the far side of the field and went cheerfully across to the sheep trough to give my tup a bonus feed. At once a sea of unsuspecting black backs were eagerly milling around and treacherously I tickled the tup. Then, when I was positioned for a good grip on the huge spreading horns, I made my lunge and grabbed with a yell that was supposed to bring Wilson and his shepherd haring across to secure the rearing animal. There lay the flaw in my plan. I grabbed, yelled and took off round the field as the tup leapt into the air, twisted, and legged it. I hit the ground flat on my face, but I hung on and was towed through the dung-laden mud at a rate of knots. Of the two men, there was no sign, I yelled, but this drove the tup to greater efforts. I lost my grip on one horn and grabbed a handful of black wet fleece. This put all my weight on one side of the animal and he spun round in ever decreasing circles. Through the splattering mud and flying hooves I could just make out the experts, standing not running, enjoying my performance. I clung on, knowing that if I let go, we'd never get near him again. At last, after I'd been tobogganed through the mud until the area looked ploughed, the two shamefaced men recovered themselves enough to stagger over to my rescue. It took their combined efforts to hold the tup and get him roped.

I heaved myself out of the mire and wiped a layer of mud from my face, I was lagged from head to foot. I stared at them accusingly.

'You took your time!' I gasped when I had the breath.

Wilson wiped the tears from his eyes.

'I'm sorry,' he choked. 'It was the sight of the flying petticoats and knickers. I just couldn't move.'

I gave him what I considered to be my most withering look and led the way out of the field.

Luckily his tup Poppet and his ewe Fifi were unloaded from Wilson's trailer without further mishap and my tup was loaded up. He gazed at me appealingly through the bars and nuzzled my hand. I patted him.

'You'll be home soon,' I reassured him, and I meant it. Poppet was a beautiful and gentle tup but he was a four-horner, the main two massive projections sticking straight up, unlike my tup's huge handlebar jobs. It was fortunate that Poppet had no evil intentions. Even so, avoiding a skewering became a major occupation, not assisted by Poppet's constant overtures of friendship.

The ewes also found they had a problem with Poppet as he continually thrust his nose under their rears in the vague hope of discovering one in season, with the result that his two horns, working on the principle of a forklift truck, lifted the horrified object of his attentions clear off the ground.

Eunice, the older ewe, was looking very heavy and even without knowing when she had been served it was obvious that lambing time was close at hand. Her udder swelled, and one day she trailed after the others with such a look of bewildered misery that I was certain she was facing mother-hood within hours rather than days.

I was uncertain of how I would cope if she experienced any difficulties. She was the most wild of the four ewes, and constantly on her guard against the approach of strangers. Like the tup, she now accepted feeding from me, although she was always wary when I lifted a hand to touch her, prepared for instant flight if I proved too pushy. I just hoped that, being one of a primitive hardy breed, she would manage without assistance. Checking her throughout the night was further complicated by unrest among the laying geese. Any sign of human intruders in the darkness would be heralded by warning screeches, alerting not only the sitting geese but also sleeping neighbours within a half-mile radius.

I checked the ewe at dusk and then decided to chance leaving her until dawn, when I hoped I would be able to observe her from the window without setting off a full-scale alarm. At six o'clock I peered out across the field to see one tiny black figure struggling to its feet while the ewe lay quietly down to deliver the second lamb quickly and without fuss. Two tiny coal-black ewe lambs!

I wondered how she would behave when I caught and examined her newborn babies. I remembered all too clearly how many weeks it had taken before I got the auction tag off her neck. And how many people it had taken to do it.

Half an hour after observing the second birth, I headed down the field prepared for battle. The ewe hadn't the size of horns of Poppet, but she was nevertheless a four-horned animal, one of the horns jutting out like that of a unicorn, and I knew to my cost it could do serious damage. Hell hath no fury greater than a mother robbed of her young!

To my amazement, she stood by, watching anxiously, but made no attempt to stop me picking up her tiny lambs. They were delightful, very small and fragile fawn-like little creatures with soft black silky curled coats. When placed on the ground, they wobbled over to mother on spindly long legs, to be greeted by a caressing nose. I had intended to leave

Eunice in the field with the others as I felt it would be too difficult to attempt to move her to the enclosure, but her apparent acceptance of my handling her newborn family decided me to attempt to move her to the small sheltered dry paddock where Piddles had her lambs

Carrying the lambs, I led the way to the gate, the ewe following nervously. So, unfortunately, were the others, led by Poppet. I opened the gate and the Clydesdales, Phantom and Clover, clearly thinking they were missing out, joined the procession. I walked through carrying the bleating lambs, and so did everyone else – except Eunice. Even four of the geese flapped through the open gate, getting under the horses' hooves and completing the choas. Eunice hung back, calling to her babies who were wriggling and kicking in my arms as I attempted to shoo everything back into the field. The muddy lane suddenly became a very crowded place, all the animals milling about, wondering where they were going and what they were getting.

Finally I dumped the tiny lambs in a pile of straw and herded everything back into the field, ready to try again. Phantom swung his huge head and snorted his approval of the new game, though Clover was not too certain that the vet would not be hovering just out of range.

Eunice, worried about her lost family, couldn't quite bring herself to be first out of the gate, though last was perhaps a possibility. At about the tenth try, I hit on a cunning plan. I let everything file out, including the new mother, led the group in a circle and let them back into the field, slamming the gate shut right under a black ewe's startled nose as she brought up the rear.

It had taken an hour to get her through that gate!

Now we were in business. I retrieved the tiny bewildered lambs from the straw and with one tucked under each arm, I led the way up the lane towards the garden, the ewe following, head-butting me every few yards to remind me that I had charge of her youngsters and she'd rather like them back.

Our arrival at the paddock caused a flurry of excitment, Piddles and her lambs lumbering forward to greet her old field mate and inspect the new members of the flock who stood nervously accepting the prodding and shoving of interested noses. Fred and Freda paced enthusiastically back and forth, surveying the crush at the gate with interest, ever hopeful that the change to their morning routine might herald a bonus breakfast.

Although the cats had made no aggressive moves towards Piddles' offspring, I was worried that they might attack the Hebridean lambs which were so much smaller and lighter than the Suffolk crosses. Finally everything was settled, and fed, and watered, and I trudged inside for my own breakfast.

Despite my fears, the cats made no attacks on the tiny frail lambs but by afternoon I was anxious about the weakest lamb's chances of survival. I watched the stronger of the twins suckling easily, but her smaller sister, although nuzzled and washed constantly by an adoring mum, did not seem to be thriving. She would frequently totter over to suckle, but the little rudder did not wag, despite the prodding nose at mother's undercarriage.

Either the lamb could not suck or the mother hadn't enough milk. I took the wobbly lamb indoors and tried to bottlefeed her, but she was too weak to pull at the tiny rubber teat, letting the milk dribble out of the corners of her mouth to soak her soft black fleece.

I phoned Lynn for advice, suggesting that I took the lamb across to her for a check up.

'Steve and I'll come right over,' she said cheerfully. 'From the sound of it, you'll have to tube-feed. We'll have a look at mum and see if she's got enough milk. Get some goat's milk and I'll bring my feeding tubes over and show you what to do. You'll need some colostrum for the first feeds.'

Tube-feeding involves inserting thin plastic piping down the throat and into the stomach. A measure of feed is then poured in carefully and the tube removed. It is a process I thought would be greeted with an equal amount of enthusiasm from both myself and the tiny lamb and the risk of killing the lamb by getting milk into the lungs was high. But the lamb was obviously going to die if it wasn't done, so the risk had to be taken. Colostrum is found in the mother's first milk flow after giving birth and it protects the newborn young from various illness. Without that first important natural protection, most young animals will die within the first few days. Orphaned or handreared animals are fed with milk taken from a foster mother within the first couple of days of giving birth and therefore receive that all important protection. Farmers often take milk from newly calved cows or newly lambed ewes and freeze it for emergencies at a later time. Fortunately a neighbour of mine had some goat's milk stored for just such a purpose and so when Lynn arrived, armed with her tubes, I had the milk ready and warmed. She immediately confirmed my fears that one lamb wasn't feeding, though it was through no fault of its own – mother was short of milk and the more dominant lamb was getting to the bar first and draining supplies.

Lamb, tube, milk and instructor ready, I received my first lesson in tube feeding. It consists of securing the struggling lamb comfortably, opening the mouth and pressing down the tongue with one hand (no mean feat in itself) while inserting the tube with the free hand and pushing it gently down the osophagus into the stomach, having first done a rough calculation on the length needed by the length of the lamb. The danger during this stage is inserting the tube into the lungs rather than the stomach, or pushing the tube too far, so damaging the internal organs in the process. To check the tube has not been pushed into the lungs, the free end has to be pressed against the cheek in order to feel the suction of the air as the organs inflate. Once certain that the tube is correctly in place, the milk is gently poured down it. If the tube has been pushed into the lungs, then a drowned lamb is the immediate result. If there are no complications, the lamb receives a nice full belly of warm milk without even the effort of sucking. However, the danger is not passed. The tube has to be pulled gently out and unless a finger is kept firmly pressed over the end, sealing it, the residue of milk in the tube can still run into the lungs.

It is a nerve-racking operation, but for speed and insuring the lamb receives a good feed before being returned to mother, it is better than struggling to feed with a bottle, which can take so long that the ewe will reject her lamb when it is returned to her.

Despite the dangers, Lynn was well experienced, and in minutes the frail little black lamb was ready to go back to mum with a full tummy and a contented sleepy smirk.

The next time, however, I was on my own and without Lynn's expert guidance. All went well though, and within three days mother had plenty of milk and my interference was no longer needed. I don't know who was the more relieved, myself or the lamb.

Although the rest of the livestock were well advanced in the trials and tribulations of motherhood, Freda still remained slim and active. Too active!

Every week produced new tricks and feats of cunning and gymastics from the cats' pen. Having come out into the open, the old hands were never tucked up securely in their sleeping den: one, usually both, were permanently on guard, waiting to attack me on sight, each day providing even greater efforts. Having learnt to rush to the wire to beat the other to the first lump of raw meat, each animal tried to outdo the other, leaping up at the wire with monkey-like agility, paws reaching through the mesh to hook the meat before it was even in range. As they became more practised, I became less comfortable. Their speed was phenomenal. As soon as I approached the enclosure two black blurs would flash towards me, taking flying leaps to spring at the mesh, front paws extended to reach through to grab at my approaching meat-filled hand. It was an unnerving experience to see the lethally hooked razor-sharp huge claws lashing towards me, and their speed resulted in constantly dropped chunks of meat as I attempted to avoid my fingers becoming part of their diet. I could gain a reprieve for a couple of days by posting the meat higher and higher through the bars, but they learnt quickly, showing an amazing intelligence and perserverance. Eventually the inevitable happened. I ran out of height, having reached the top line of mesh for posting the meat while Fred and Freda leap-frogged up and over each other's backs with amazing dexterity to hang gibbon-like from the roof while reaching through to hook their supper.

One evening Fred surpassed himself by leaping above my head height to grab at a particularly large chunk of meat I was pushing through the wire. As the huge front paw lashed out I let go of the meat and leapt out of range in the nick of time, having failed to squash the pigeon-size piece of beef through the hole. To Fred's horror, the meat was firmly jammed, one half sticking invitingly just out of reach. He hung by one front and one back paw and attempted to pull the chunk towards him with the remaining two paws. The meat was well and truly stuck however, and even with the additional use of teeth, it would not pass through the tiny gap. Furious and frustrated, he tore and ripped at the bloody flesh, only succeeding in pulling shreds through, which he promptly dropped, concentrating his efforts on the main chunk. Freda sat below him positively delighted with the whole episode, eagerly scoffing back the juicy fragments as they showered about her. Manna from Heaven! By now Fred had worked himself into a positive frenzy. Nothing mattered to him but retrieving the main part of the lump of beef. He actually hung on to the roof with just one front paw while he twisted and turned, swinging against the mesh, three strong legs thrusting through the bars to pull the chunk towards him, his black-whiskered face squashed against the mesh, his teeth bared as he snatched at the rapidly disintergrating morsel. Finally, with a scream of triumph, he pulled the remains through and with a satisfied growl dropped to the ground and carried it away to his eating shelf. It was a hard won but hollow victory, however, for the once prize lump had shrunk to a mere shredded crumb, Freda having devoured the bulk of it as it had rained about her.

The episode had taught Fred nothing except that he had the ability to hang on with just one paw, a talent he continued to put into practice at feeding times.

The new cat, Kelly, still remained unseen and unheard, but her food was taken every night and her latrine straw heap was used with healthy regularity, so I presumed all was well with her.

As well as the kinder spring weather bringing new arrivals in the field, the ewes proudly parading their lambs around, carefully avoiding the family groups of geese with their newly hatched fluffy balls of goslings that waddled through the rushes, I also had a rush of visitors. I had changed publisher and was discussing a book about the Kellas cats with my new editor, Tony Colwell. He drove up with his wife from London, to meet me and the cats in the flesh. He didn't say so, but I think he was eager to ascertain the animals really existed. Far from avoiding humans, Fred and Freda now delighted in a frenzied attack at the sight of strangers, leaping at the wire and lunging at the startled visitors as a great game. After the first frenzy Fred's party piece was to sit quietly studying the strangers with silent fascination, his orange eyes almost hypnotic, until the moment the visitor relaxed and turned away. Then the massive tom would fling himself once more at the wire mesh with a loud spitting growl, making the stranger jump. After each attack, he would settle back with a satisfied smirk and wait for the next unsuspecting turn of a back.

Tony and his wife were suitably impressed by Fred's intractable display. Later over lunch, when I asked what they thought about the terrible pair, Tony said the cats were everything I had said and more!

His wife nodded. 'They certainly aren't domestic cats stuffed with steroids,' she said quite seriously.

Now that was something I had never even considered, that people might suspect I was giving ordinary moggies a physical boost. It produced visions of Fred in his hut doing his daily dozen and pumping iron to build up the muscles. Mind you, he certainly was on a steak diet.

My next visitor was Andrew Kitchener from the Royal Museum of Scotland. Andrew had been instrumental in my acquisition of Fred and Freda and had been one of the few people to see the animals when they were in the Highland Wildlife Park. I was curious to see how he felt the animals were adapting to their new home.

On seeing strangers approaching the two cats licked their lips in anticipation of the fun ahead and went into their 'Get off my patch' routine.

'It's all just macho display,' he said, studying the animals' ferocity. 'They are just putting it on. They aren't a bit bothered by our presence.'

I agreed. 'There's no hatred in the eyes now,' I said. 'There used to be, but now it's all just for effect.' Fred sunk into a sitting position and stared at us with an almost hurt expression. We weren't playing the game. Freda paced alongside him, frustrated by our lack of reaction.

Andrew nodded. 'They certainly are behaving differently here than they did in the wildlife park. They are obviously quite content and settled with you.'

'Why do you think they've changed in such a short time?' I asked. After all, I had had them for only five months; the wildlife park had had them for years.

Andrew shrugged. 'This is possibly the first time they've had a chance to form a relationship with one person. They also haven't had hordes of people disturbing them and you've taken the time and trouble to relate to them.' Fred gazed back as if fascinated by this discussion of his behaviour. 'And,' added Andrew, 'it will probably be the first time they have been involved with a woman. That alone could make a difference. Your approach would have been more gentle, your voice softer than they were used to.'

Whatever the reason, he agreed the cats were thriving and all looked well for the breeding programme. Then came the main reason for his visit – collecting the specimens for the genetic study. I unpacked the five dead Kellas specimens from the freezer, together with two road casualty otters and a cat casualty bat I had collected for the museum. For the first time in seven years I had an almost empty freezer. All I was left with was a road casualty barn owl, a stoat and a cat casualty robin that I had thought too beautiful to be thrown away. 'Are these any use for mounting in displays at the museum?' I asked.

Andrew nodded. 'Oh, we can use them for study skins or display,' he said, and I had an empty freezer.

As we loaded the frozen cat carcases into his car I felt strangely sad, the specimens were the result of eight years of my life, eight years of persuading gamekeepers and farmers to contact me if a Kellas was seen or killed, eight years of driving round talking to people, tracking through forests and woodland, eight years of trying to gain scientific interest in the beautiful black beasts of the Highlands.

Standing in the lane, staring at the distant snow-capped mountains as I watched Andrew's cat-laden car bump along the rutted track to head south, I felt a sense of loss rather than achievement. I had fought to get the Kellas cats recognised as something worth studying rather than something to be dismissed out of hand. Now all I had worked for was happening: a prestigious museum was undertaking an active research programme into the origins of the cats, to discover their genetic make-up. But now that the scientific establishment had decided to involve itself, my work was almost done. Soon I would no longer be an important part of the research for others would now take over. It was almost like sending a child to school for the first time; the infant would be stepping into a bigger and more interesting outside world and the mother-child relationship would never be the same again. Other influences would be brought to bear. I felt it was like this with the Kellas cats. Now that I had handed over the specimens, the whole research programme had passed out of my control.

Yet it wasn't a bereavement; it was a change. The scientists now had carcases to play around with, but I had the living creatures. A live spitting grumpy Fred was far more interesting to watch than a limp bleeding carcase.

I looked at the forest-clothed hills around me and thought of the Kellas cats hunting, fighting and rearing their young in the wilderness of the Highlands. I had handed over my work and part of my life, but in return I was embarking on a whole new experience.

My new challenge was to understand how the living Kellas mind functioned, and if possible to obtain one young enough to accept an even closer relationship with me. Fred and Freda trusted me but they did not like me. Could a kitten with no experience of the cruelty of the human race, could such a small creature learn to trust and even return affection to me?

Let the world of science play around with their bones and blood, I had something much more interesting to occupy my time.

13

Spring Arrivals

Spring settled its grip on the Highlands and the bleak barren
hills began to shimmer with fresh green as the trees finally
burst into leaf. Along the river bank the drifts of dark green
spears of snowflake leaves were overwhelmed and buried
beneath the larger knife blades of daffodils, their trumpets
nodding in the cool breeze, flashes of sunlight on the mossy
banks. In the sheep-cropped grass across the hillside slopes
the violets peeped out from beneath their dark canopy of
leaves and the primroses clustered like pools of pale light,
casting golden shadows beneath the overhanging rocks and
tree roots. The banks of the burn and the river were carpeted
with the fragile white and pale pink stars of the wood
anemones through which pushed the underpile of buttercup-
yellow celandine. Along the water's edge and in the marshy
areas were spreading clumps of brassy kingcups and the
misty blue haze of speedwell and forget-me-nots. The trees
were not to be outdone by the ground around their roots. The
spreading wild cherry dipped its branches, heavy with
blossom, and the Rowan and elder were hazy with frothy
flowers.

Every walk along the river bank or up the hill to the forest
produced new delights – a russet gold stoat flashing across
the path intent on the scent of vole or woodmouse, a hare

kicking its furry heels in the air, leaping and capering through the rushes, zig-zagging across the fields in a frenzy of spring madness. Overhead a solitary squirrel could sometimes be glimpsed, though such sightings were rare and precious – a small red lean body with a skimpy fluffy russet tail, very unlike the heavier plump grey squirrels of the south. The roe deer were more often spotted in the shadows of the larch trees, small dainty creatures, the enemy of forester and farmer alike, browsing on the new tree shoots, their huge brown eyes watching for any sign of danger, their noses twitching for every scent, the large ears flicking away the buzzing insects.

Rabbits grazed carelessly in the clearings and fields, oblivious to the constant danger from a hunting fox or a buzzard. The beauty of the Highland forests are the lack of people passing through them. It is frequently years between thinnings with the result that few human feet tread the forest paths, making the animals living within the tree shadows confident, secure in the cover of pine thickets. The variety of birdlife to be seen is tremendous, sea, water, forest and moorland species all living alongside each other in the varied scenic countryside.

Along the shallow swiftly flowing river, smart black and white dippers bob and weave across the mossy boulders, their beaks probing and digging in the crevices for small crustaceans. In the fields lapwings and oyster-catchers crouch motionless, often sheltering their pebble-like eggs. The finches begin to disperse in the spring after a winter of surviving in large flocks, and the bright yellow siskins squabble with green finches, gold finches and chaffinches while robbing the farmer and gardener of their newly sown seeds.

These are the everyday sights of the Highland countryside, but each country walk provides a new sight or experience. One day I watched a buzzard flapping through the trees, its huge wings lazily beating just a couple of feet off the ground as it weaved its way through the closely packed trees. It seemed an impossible feat to fly through the narrowly spaced trunks with its broad wingspan but it never faltered in its flight pattern, continuing its slow steady progress without a change of rhythm. Why a bird normally seen floating high on the warm thermals should choose a passage just a couple of feet above the forest floor I have no idea. I just watched it until it disappeared into the shadows, though I could still hear the steady beat of its great wings long after it was lost from view.

A regular visitor to the burn was a heron. He stood hunched, his long neck curled, his eye glinting beadily as he watched for the unwary trout or passing frog. For some reason, my dog Mut had developed an almost pathological hatred for the heron, though what the imagined grievance was I never discovered. His great delight was to disturb the poor creature, sending it flapping up into the sky in utter panic, though even that was not enough for Mut who would then proceed to chase the great bird across the field, barking furiously at the sky-born figure until hauled back and put on the lead for his pains. Other visitors were less churlishly treated. A pair of mallard ducks arrived in my bottom field one day, obviously scouting the area for nesting possibilities. Mut treated the pair with mild curiosity, and soon the ducks stopped their panic flights at the sight of us, the small brown female waddling purposefully along, quack-nagging her brightly coloured mate as he trailed behind her, listening to her strident quacks with a cowed expression.

Then in May, only the male remained in view, waddling worriedly across the horse-churned bog. It was obvious the female was sitting somewhere in the rushes but I decided to leave her in peace to attempt to rear her brood. I just hoped she was well hidden from the pair of foxes which frequently crossed the field and had dined on my own ducks, geese and chickens on more than one occasion.

Other regular carnivores that posed a threat to the maternal duck were the mink that hunted along the stream. Mut frequently picked up their scent along the river bank, whining with excitment as he splashed through the shallows, quartering the stoney ground, thrusting his muzzle into every nook and cranny on a mink search. Luckily for Mut's questing nose, the chocolate brown poachers were well hidden, sleeping off their night's hunting in deep tunnels, only occasionally glimpsed splashing along the water's edge or bounding across the path.

Living in the countryside, one is very conscious of the daily life and death battle for existence, a balance that is disturbed only by man's interference. The farmer and the gamekeeper wage war on the poor old fox because of his occasional sins against stock, though in the north-east Highlands their solution is a personal private feud; no traditional redcoats and packs of hunting dogs calling blood lust sport, just the warring farmer or gamekeeper, his lamp, stealth and gun pitted against the natural cunning and intelligence of the beast. In such circumstances, the hunter does not sacrifice his comfortable warm bed for the chill night air of the hillside unless his quarry has made its presence felt by attacks on his farm or bird stocks. The fox that hunts only the rabbit or the hare assists the farmer to protect his arable crops and therefore is left alone to live in peace and harmony until it makes the mistake of turning its culinary attentions to man's property. A fair arrangement to all but the poor old bunnies. Deer are more of a target. A browsing small herd can decimate a newly planted forest almost overnight, but once the trees have reached survival size even the deer can live in comparative peace alongside the foresters, grazing the undergrowth and clearing the scrubby hillside to provide space for grass to grow.

It is in such a balance between farming and nature that the Kellas cats live, hunt and fall foul of keepers. Like the wildcat and feral domestic cat, it is difficult even to attempt an estimate of the number of animals living wild, the only guide being the number killed or captured. Even the number killed is uncertain. Some estates and keepers are willing to take the time and trouble to contact me if the cats are snared or shot on their land, while others are simply throwing the carcases aside without wanting to be bothered with the effort involved in contacting either myself or the museum.

One farmer told Andrew Kitchener that he frequently killed the 'devil cats' along the west coast. They weren't wildcats or domestics, he explained, but demons of cats, more ferocious than the ordinary wildcat. They were different, and terrifying, and no one would attempt to catch one alive.

As I watched Fred and Freda at feeding time, I could well understand the farmer's sentiments, the snarling bundles of spitting fury hurling themselves at the wire in a frenzy of lashing claws and bared teeth. Yet despite the regular onslaught when the pen was approached, they would afterwards sink back satisfied, their eyes shuttered and calm, to wash themselves calmly, though they were always alert for any movement, ready to resume their murderous attack at a moment's notice.

Their behaviour towards one another was still changing, Freda constantly striking out at Fred, who backed off, swearing, but did not retaliate against her furious and unprovoked attacks. She was now frequently taking the first chunk of meat, often snatching it out of the bigger cat's mouth and scampering off leaving the huge tom looking shocked at the audacity of the deed. Although she did not appear to be spreading around the middle I suspected the tom's tolerance – a marked contrast to his earlier behaviour towards her – might be the result of her pregnancy. There was still no evidence of affection between them, as there is between domestic cats. They never had mutual grooming sessions or even sniffed noses as most cats do. Instead it was as if they led separate lives within the same space. They slept in the same sleeping den and often sat side by side sunning themselves on the roof of their den but they never actually seemed to make physical contact, always keeping just that little bit apart like a married couple after a tiff.

One day they had good reason to be disgruntled. I went

out unexpectly at tea time and didn't return till after dark. Mandy had agreed to feed the animals, as frequently she did for me. But the cats were always my task and not in the girl's feeding routine, so horses, sheep, goats, geese, hens, peacock and rabbit all got their supper, but the poor cats were forgotten. It was too dark to feed them when I got back, so they had a hungry night until half past six the following morning. If Fred and Freda were more than a little miffed at the delayed serving, the wait had a useful side. As I walked into the paddock I saw a lean blur of black as Fred leapt across his compound and vanished behind Kelly's sleeping den with a crash. Then I realised that Fred was sitting studying me from his shed while Freda was emerging from their den. The long black blur had been Kelly, who had been caught unawares sitting on top of her sleeping den. It was the first time I had seen her since she had been released into the enclosure. Unfortunately the sighting had been too quick to note anything about her, but the speed at which she moved obviously meant she was in good health and fully recovered from her injuries. To move that fast indicated she had adapted to life on three legs. The fact that I had mistaken her for the tom rather than Freda also suggested she was much larger than the first female.

The following afternoon, as I was walking down the lane, I spotted her again in daylight. A black-whiskered face peered through the wire at me for seconds before again vanishing speedily into the shelter of her den. It was reminiscent of Freda gathering courage to be seen in daylight. At first there were just fleeting tantalising glimpses of a black blur. Kelly, not having been in captivity for years, would take a little longer to risk exposure, but it certainly looked hopeful that within months, maybe weeks, she would be joining the queue at supper time.

I considered it was time to think of building a hide in an attempt to film her.

Priority, though, was the separate pen for Freda. If she was about to produce young, everything had to be constructed well before the birth to give her time to settle into the maternity wing.

Cash was the overwhelming problem. I had run out of the donated spot-welded wire mesh, Kelly's compound having used all my reserves. Then I had a stroke of luck. An old Victorian Distillery was being demolished nearby and a small pile of spot-welded mesh panels suddenly appeared among a pile of scrap metal. They were a bit bent and twisted, but were definitely salvageable, despite their gungy coats of old gloss paint. I knew the lads working on the site and before long stage one of the ante-natal pen was under way.

However, obtaining the mesh was not the same thing as constructing the enclosure. Building Kelly's pen had been difficult enough with a macho Fred leaping around trying to inflict maximum damage on maximum person; this time I had a furious Freda to contend with as well. It was not a prospect to stir the soul with confidence.

I also had to decide on to which of the two remaining sides of the enclosure to add the additional wing. The original planned site was now of course taken up by Kelly's pen across the front of the main enclosure. The rear was totally occupied by the shed that took up the full width of the space. That left only the two sides, one of which was partially boarded across and the other was the section I used for feeding the terrible pair.

It would be difficult to add the extension to the boarded area as the ground was uneven, knee-high in nettles and thistles and overgrown with alder trees with their extensive tap roots. At the same time, it would produce real problems to block off the area where Fred and Freda were fed. To avoid being hooked by lashing claws was difficult enough without room to manoeuvre; to have to feed the cats from the narrow passageway between the inner and outer doorway would be almost impossible. I decided it had to be the boarded side, despite the rough ground.

Deciding where to site the extension was still not the same as acquiring all the materials and getting the task completed.

Other projects were taking up a great deal of my time, so daily I studied Freda's waistline for any sign of expansion and kept putting off the extension as not being urgent.

But if her waistline was not showing signs of pregnancy, her relationship with Fred was definitely altering drastically. She lashed out viciously at him without the slightest provocation and he would retreat before her furious onslaught. She always snatched the food first and raced off to her den with it. Fred spent most of his time sunning himself on the roof of the den or else lying in a flopped heap on the floor of the shed. One morning I surprised him sprawled on his back, his four feet stretched up in the air in a quite ludicrous manner. He was so deeply asleep that I had reached the wire before he was aware of me and he rolled over and fell off the step in shock. His indignation at my intrusion resulted in the first pistol shot *Phaah*! I'd heard for a while. I felt it was his embarrassment rather than anger that being was voiced in the violent spit.

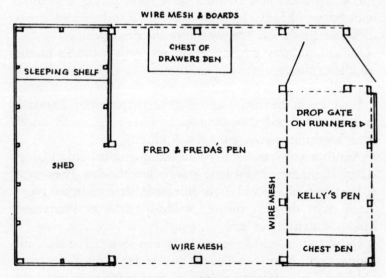

LAYOUT OF KELLAS CATS ENCLOSURE

I described the changing relationship between the two cats to Andrew Kitchener when he phoned.

'I think she might be pregnant, judging by the way she's constantly attacking him, but there's no sign of a spreading waistline yet,' I said.

'How long has she been behaving like this?'

'About a month I suppose. Poor old Fred is terrified to move.'

'Maybe she is pregnant.'

Wildcat pregnancy was about sixty days in duration; if Freda was expecting, I still had enough time to prepare the maternity unit.

Two days later Freda's snatching claws hooked the first piece of meat before Fred's disgusted eyes and spitting and snarling in triumph, she carried it to the centre of the enclosure. Fred hooked the next piece through the mesh and lugged it wearily off to the security of the shed. Freda ripped her piece into bite-size chunks, lashing at Fred's rear as he passed, apparently just for the pleasure of it. Fred flinched and scuttled off in a crablike movement, giving his mate a wide berth. I heard a high-pitched squeal and glanced across to where Freda was peering out of the den opening.

Something was wrong. Freda was still standing in the middle of the pen.

Fred?

Fred was in the shed. I stared at the den entrance. The dark grey head bobbed about and gazed out at the sunlit world from bright blue innocent eyes. A kitten!

Another yowl and I saw two more chubby little figures staggering around in the long grass below the den. They were at least four weeks old, with fine, soft, dark charcoal grey-black coats showing distinct wildcat markings. Freda and Fred had a family at last!

I sank down on to the cool grass in shock. No sign, no sound, nothing had revealed the cats' secret. No wonder poor old Fred had suffered his mate's aggression; no wonder he had taken up residence in the shed.

The two kittens wobbled and toddled around, feeling their legs on the ground for the first time. The third one hung out of the entrance, watching its litter mates explore, desperate to join them but afraid to take that first all important step. It scrabbled on the edge of the ledge, its huge paws showing massive light coloured claws as it pawed at the rough wood. Freda gave a low rumbling sound and the kits responded, the pair on the ground tottering across to their mother on shaky legs. She sniffed them and then knocked one over on its back with her head. She opened her mouth and made a biting movement downwards. I held my breath. Was she simply trying to grab it and lift it by the scruff or was she biting its throat, killing it because I had disturbed the family. Was this how the others had died? There was nothing I could do but watch. Any sudden movement would almost certainly seal the kitten's fate. The kit lay still and limp. Freda gripped the neck and hauled it up, straddling the dangling body like she did her food. The kitten squeaked a slight protest and I sighed with relief. She was only carrying the little body, not killing it. She half dragged the kit back to the den entrance where the third one still scrabbled, trying to gain courage to face the unknown. Freda tried to lift the kitten into the den but it was too large and kept jamming against the side, its mother constantly dropping it in disgust and readjusting her grip to try again. Quietly I slipped round to the back of the pen and unfastened the cord holding the cover in position over the entrance, jerking it up and enlarging the hole, giving Freda more room to move. She sprang up and dropped the kitten into the gap just as the third kitten overbalanced and fell out, hanging for a moment by its front paws before dropping down on to the soft grass. Freda swore and went to grab it and shove it roughly back into the den. I moved quietly away and left her to her family problems.

The next morning I tip-toed out at about six to see if all was well. I was desperately afraid that now the kittens had been revealed to human eyes Freda would turn on them and kill them. The long grass was wet with dew and the pale summer sun filtered down through the misty morning haze. Fred was sitting washing himself on the den roof. Freda was standing on her hind legs, watching me approach, obviously hopeful for a breakfast bonus. Three chubby kittens tumbled and wobbled through the grass beneath the den, playing silently, their wide blue eyes showing their interest in the new exciting daylight world around them. Wind-rustled grass blades were pounced on and murdered with delight, and siblings' tails were an irresistible challenge.

Freda snarled and spat, warning me to watch my step, but I settled down on the damp grass to watch quietly. It was the first time I was able to see all three kittens together and compare them.

They were unlike anything I had expected. They were not black but a very dark smokey grey, with a sooty sheen to the fur on the body and a silvery blue-grey sheen to the head and paws. Clearly discernible were the wildcat markings – thin dark chocolate brown stripes across the back and sides, the banded tail and the distinctive M on the forehead. Their heads, ears and paws appeared comically large for their chubby bodies. Their eyes were large, round and a beautiful blue. They played like household kittens with one notable difference: they made virtually no sound as they rolled and tumbled across the grass. No squeals and yowls, or rumbling growls. Watching them was like watching a silent movie, all the action was there but the sound was switched off.

I could understand how the kittens had remained secret. Obviously wildcat kits have an instinct to remain silent and hidden in their den, no sound alerting a passing predator of their existence. I spoke softly to Freda, reassuring her that I meant her kittens no harm. Fred sat glumly watching his offspring playing. There was no hint of dislike in his expression, only a tired henpecked weariness. Clearly Fred considered family life not all it was cracked up to be. I suspected he rather regretted the sudden change in his circumstances. He jumped down off the den roof and slowly ambled across to the shed. Freda took her attention off me to dart across and belt poor old Fred across the rear. The tom reared up and spat his protest at the unnecessary violence, but retreated backwards away from his shrewish mate and sat down, looking across to me with a helpless expression on his face.

I couldn't believe the quiet subdued Fred. It seemed unnatural. Freda stood, fur on end, warning him to watch his step. A kitten wobbled across and went to suckle. Freda remembered me and whipped across to give me a token warning attack. Fred and I were being kept firmly in our places. The kitten, still firmly attached to mum's teat, came with her, hanging on to her undercarriage. Then Freda settled down next to me and with a token maternal lick to her kitten, allowed it to feed. I was amazed. She was actually choosing a spot next to me in which to relax and suckle her youngster. Another kitten staggered across to the restaurant. Freda welcomed it with a low rumbled greeting. I sat quiet, hardly daring to breathe.

That Freda would actually feed the kittens in my presence was amazing enough, but to feed them next to me was the greatest compliment she could pay me. Despite her furious and constant attacks on me, she was showing that she trusted me completely.

That trust suddenly became even more apparent. Freda stood up and walked across to the den, dragging one kitten with her, leaving one behind. There she sat by the third kitten and watched me with calm golden eyes. The kitten by me made no attempt to follow her. It settled down in a tiny furry ball, its back pushed against the wire, contentedly dozing. Freda also settled comfortably.

I could have stroked the soft fur through the bars, I felt the terrible temptation to do so, but resisted. I had worked so hard to gain the trust of the adult cats but I could lose it in an instant with one false move. I stood up slowly and moved quietly away.

The Kellas family watched me go.

The first Kellas kittens had been born in captivity. The scientists were working on the dead Kellas specimens in order to determine their origins. I had a different task. I had to help the cats rear their kittens into healthy adult cats, the first ever captive bred Kellas.

And then what?

Would it be possible to find a sanctuary where game-keepers were not trigger happy, a place where the Kellas cats could live in peace, mate and rear their young in the wild as nature had intended?

Whatever the scientific findings, the Kellas cats were beautiful, wild free spirits. With so many species being destroyed by man, perhaps just one could be helped instead.

I stood and watched the cats from a distance. Demon cats they were not. Fairy cats perhaps.

14

To the Rescue

The kits had strange round flat faces, quite unlike the elfin pointed faces of domestic kittens. Their eyes were small and round, with an almost blank hypnotic stare, the pupil showing only as a thin black streak in a grey-blue iris. Their small flattened ears were set to the side of the head. They were sturdily built and had tiny rudder-like tails. Their coat colour was the most striking and unexpected feature.

All three kittens were indistinguishable from each other; there was no dilution or even shading difference discernable in the coats. It was difficult to be certain of their age but, using the domestic kitten's development as a guide, I estimated them to be about four weeks old. They were strong and powerful, though at first a little wobbly on their back legs, frequently using their heavily clawed front feet for hauling themselves in and out of the den entrance, revealing remarkable strength as the entrance was about eighteen inches above the ground.

Freda was extremely protective towards the kits, rushing at the mesh, claws lashing out, spitting furiously at any approach. The kittens fled underneath the den at the first sign of danger, sometimes peeping out through the long grass, curious despite their caution. As they became more accustomed to the outside world, they began to play leaping on siblings' tails and windblown leaves. As they gained in strength and courage, they began to tumble, roll and scuffle, boxing with their front paws and kicking with their back legs, but they seemed to have less personal contact than domestic kittens at play. They were more likely to make a concentrated attack together on a thistle leaf or a grass blade than on each other. Stalking and pouncing seemed to be the main occupation rather than paw to paw combat. They would often work as a team, creeping slowly up to a chosen target, surrounding it in a ring and leaping in almost at the same moment to murder a dock leaf or massacre a wandering beetle.

As they became more confident they began to ignore me. Sometimes Freda would allow them to approach the mesh, although her watchful eye was always on them and a warning spit was usually aimed in my direction to warn me not to push my luck. If she was uncertain or worried, she would spring across, snarling furiously, and then attempt to grab the unfortunate kitten by the neck and carry it out of the danger zone.

Her protective instincts were not aided by the size and weight of her offspring. She seldom succeeded in grabbing the scruff of the neck, usually knocking the protesting kitten over and attempting to get it by the throat. At first the kits were small enough that their whole heads almost disappeared into their mother's mouth, but the exercise looked more dangerous than it actually was. Visitors to see the family would look white-faced and horrified as they visualised the kits having their heads bitten off.

The first time it happened in front of me I shared their horror, thinking that I was witnessing a death strike. This was not an irrational fear. It was known that either Freda or Fred had killed at least one litter. It was a scene I was to become familar with over the following weeks. Every time I approached, poor Freda became desperate, rushing from one to another of her brood, grabbing at one, then dropping it to try and pick up a different kit. The kits found the daylight world much more exciting and interesting than their warm dark den and as mum grabbed and hauled each kit back to safety, the others constantly made successful escape bids, tumbling to freedom past her frantic head as she attempted to shove each one back into the den.

While Freda was tearing her fur out in frustration, Fred looked very subdued and unhappy. He usually sat slouched in the shed, watching the antics of his offspring with a jaded eye, a shadow of his former macho glory. If he attempted to slink across the enclosure, Freda would flash across in a black blur, paws striking out, claws extended, and he would reverse back swiftly, rearing up to defend himself from the lashing front legs but capitulating almost instantly and dropping down to crawl backwards away from the furious onslaught.

As the kits became more ambitious and widened their territory around the den, so poor Fred became more restricted in his movements, eventually being confined to the shed and the den roof. He took his life in his paws to cross the disputed territory from the shed doorway to within springing distance of the den roof. To add to his woes, he suffered an attack of virus infection, his eyes weeping as he snuffled and snorted through his blocked up nasal passages.

I was worried that the kits would become ill through exposure to the virus at such an early age, but luckily they appeared free of the symptoms. Freda also gave no indication that she was suffering from the virus, which was surprising as the staff at the Highland Wildlife Park had told me that all the wildcats had caught the disease and there was no cure, the virus being resilient against antibiotics. I had suggested that the kittens might be born with a natural immunity but the idea was dismissed by the experts. Yet the kits remained clear-eyed and clean-nosed, unlike their poor dad who sniffed and snuffled in a quite revolting way for weeks, a permanent stream of muscus bubbling from his nostrils.

Apart from my concern over infection, there was still the constant fear that the huge male would get fed up with the constant harrassment by his mate and decide to take matters into his own paws. The death of at least one earlier litter, if not more, hung heavily on me, having been unable to separate the pair before the birth. Certainly it appeared that the kits had already passed the most dangerous period before I even saw them, but I also knew from past experience that a domestic tom could turn, for no apparent reason, and kill kittens as old as six or seven weeks.

It was almost certain that any former Kellas litters met their end at a much earlier age for, apart from the one reported sighting of a kit peering out of the den entrance, no one had seen any evidence of kittens during their years of captivity in the Highland Wildlife Park. At an estimate of one month old my three kits were out and about frequently during the day, staggering around on stiff stubby legs or peering out of the den entrance, their blue eyes wide with the wonder of the great outside. If they had survived that long in the wildlife park, then they could not have remained unnoticed. After about an hour's exploration, they would wobble back to be grabbed by the throat and uncermoniously dumped into the den by a harrassed Freda, or else they would haul themselves up, digging their needle sharp little claws into the soft wood as they scrabbled up the front of the cupboard to balance precariously on the ledge before dropping out of sight inside.

Freda would usually go in with them, obviously to suckle them for a few minutes, then she would slip quietly out to leave her kits sleeping, renewing their energy for the next bout of freedom.

When Freda entered or left the den, the kits made no sound of either greeting or protest. Most young animals greet their mother with identifying calls, but the kits remained totally silent while Freda made constant low-pitch conversational sounds, clearly to reassure them about her presence.

Within a couple of weeks of their first taste of freedom, the kittens had really found their feet, scampering about the enclosure and dashing up and down the sides of the den with boundless enthusiasm, to the constant panic of their worried mother. Fred seemed to accept the kittens scurrying around him with a calm laid back air. He showed no more than a mild interest in their activities, but neither did he reveal any annoyance when they pounced on his swishing tail or dashed across his slumbering back. Even Freda eventually gave up her constant panics and relaxed her guard although her attention was permanently on her kits. That she trusted me, despite her frequent attacks, was made obvious when, on occasion, she would come over to the side of the wire where I sat studying them, lean on the mesh next to me and contentedly suckle the kits. These were moments of pure magic, to sit in the grass on a warm summer's day and watch the kittens tumble on to their backs with their chubby paws waving in the air as they kneaded at their mother's belly, their pink mouths firmly clasped on the nipples, their eyes tightly closed, their tummies swelling. Most kittens or cubs drone in contented rumbling purrs while feeding but the Kellas kits suckled lustily in complete silence. It was the same during play. They would bounce and pounce, leap and jump all over each other, but it was like watching television with the sound turned off. All the movements were there, lips curled back in mock snarls, but never any actual sound.

My days spent watching the kittens were not wasted. The weeds grew high in the garden, the housework went undone, but I was learning about the Kellas family and what I learnt seemed to be of value to wildcat research. When Dr Kitchener came to see the family I asked him if wildcat kittens were silent. He admitted he didn't know. Later he phoned me to say that someone down south who was rearing captive wildcat kittens had also noticed the kittens never cried out. Silence was obviously a wildcat trait.

It was a happy time. The kits grew strong, Freda obviously loved motherhood and Fred seemed very gentle, even if unenthusiastic about his youngsters. I spent hours trying to sex the kits, studying their rears every time they rolled on to their backs with their tiny bottoms in range. I was sure there was one male and one female, but I was totally frustrated in my attempts to sex the third. They never all rolled over together, and they were so alike I could not tell which ones I had already sexed. If I was right, and one was a male, then he was unrelated to the three legged female, Kelly, so he could be paired off with her when he grew up, giving us two breeding pairs of cats.

The weeks became months. In August I was due to go south to Devon in order to do some research for my book on the Exmoor Beast. By then the kittens were almost four months old and two had already learnt to take small pieces of meat from my hand at feeding times. The third held back, watching the antics of its siblings with wide curious eyes but no obvious hunger pangs. I was sure the shy kit was the female and perhaps less forward than the others who might both be males. They still all looked identical. Their coats were becoming black but the chocolate stripes were still in evidence. Their eyes had changed from the sky blue of babyhood to a strange blue orange mixture that stared constantly at everyone and everything. As the two meat-eaters developed the taste for beef chunks, they began to take terrible risks, pouncing on Freda's and Fred's suppers, firmly embedding themselves into the glistening bloody chunks and hanging on for dear life. That was exactly what I feared they would lose as the result of such daredevil thieving. To my amazement, however, after the first disbelieving shocked growl and a brief tug of war, the adult cats gave in every time, allowing the reckless youngsters to haul away triumphantly the spoils of war. It seemed that nothing could go wrong.

I was away for just a week. When I returned, it was to a scene of carnage. Only two kits remained in the enclosure and one was limping badly with either an injured hip or back leg. Of the third kitten, there remained only a tell-tale scrap of black fur and a tiny tail amongst the debris on the shed floor.

Sadly I accepted that in my absence the two meat-eating kittens had gone too far in their antics and incurred the wrath of either one or both parents. It was a situation I had prepared for during the first weeks, but I never suspected it would happen at such a late stage in the kittens' development. It was a bitter blow, made worse by the fear for the life of the injured kit.

Every day I steeled myself for the worst, but there seemed to be no recurrence of whatever had triggered the attack. The healthy kitten played with its lame littermate and still bounced and plagued its parents at every opportunity. The injured kitten was also quite active despite its damaged leg, playing and wobbling around, making any attempt of mine to get it out of the enclosure impossible. I was afraid that the adults would eventually kill it simply because it was lame, yet all through my constant vigil I could see no evidence of bad temper from the adults towards either kit. If it hadn't have been for the sad little remains of the lost kit, I would never have suspected there had been any violence within the family.

The beginning of September brought a foretaste of the oncoming winter. A chill wind stripped the leaves from the trees before they had a chance to don their gaudy russet reds and gold and the lambs huddled miserably, heads down, fleeces dripping, their first taste of the harsh weather to come. The horses clustered under the conifers, their ample rumps and soggy tails facing the wind. The cats no longer sunned themselves, making it difficult to monitor the kits' condition. The injured kitten seldom left the den.

Saturday saw a slight improvement on the previous four days' weather though it remained wet, windy and abnormally cold for the time of year. It felt more like January than early September and all the livestock was suffering. I tried to suppress the feelings of unease at the continued absence of one kitten. Perhaps due to the weather, it was remaining inside the den. After all, I could see it was alive for it frequently peeped out at me through the den entrance, and it didn't look ill. Its eyes were alert and bright, its fur glossy. Yet I was sure there was something wrong. There seemed to be an expression of bewilderment in the golden orange eyes, not illness or fear, but something I could not quite understand.

Then on the fourth day after, I had first noticed the kitten's absence from the enclosure, I took out the evening meat to find both adults and one kitten in the shed. The other kitten was still in the den, peeping out at me through the rainlashed fading light. I fed Freda and Fred as usual, and they both dashed back into the shed with their spoils, obviously preferring the open shelter to the smaller den. The first kitten still remained in a lying position on the shed floor while the other studied me from the den.

I was surprised. Normally the active kitten would venture out to take a piece of meat, or else just toddle over to stare at me while gathering up the courage to remove a chunk in front of its possessive parents. Since the death of the third kitten the junior rush for food was a thing of the past.

Then I realised that, with the other three cats in the shed, the adults concentrating on their supper and the second kitten framed in the den entrance, this might be a safe opportunity to sneak into the enclosure for a quick look at the kit in the den. I could drop in a piece of meat in case it couldn't get out for its food. It was risky. Normally the sound of the wooden door creaking would have Freda and Fred out of the shed at an amazing speed to rush the opening door with a full frontal attack. But with Fred more laid back perhaps the gusting wind would mask the sound as neither of the cats would expect me to enter the enclosure after feeding them. I decided to take the chance. I moved quietly round to the outer door and opened it slowly, slipping into the inner passage. The next move was the most difficult as the cats knew the sound of the latch and associated it with the door being opened. I moved it gently, with as little noise as possible, and opening the door slowly, squeezed through. The kitten in the den still stared at me quite calmly with no sign of distress. As I peered down at it the kit didn't spit or pull back, but simply gazed up at me trustingly.

I felt a dreadful sense of frustration. If I had had a pair of gauntlets I was sure I could have just reached in and grabbed it by the scruff and been out of the pen before the adults were even aware anything had happened. With the right equipment, it would have been so easy, but with just my bare hands I could do nothing. The kitten was five months old, powerfully built, already with an impressive set of teeth and claws. Although it obviously trusted me to stand close to it, there was no way it was going to allow me to put my hand into the den, I would have been ripped to pieces in seconds. I tossed in a small piece of meat and retreated through the gate slamming it shut just as Fred came hurtling out of the shed in spitting fury as he realised he had been tricked. Freda followed, almost trampling the second kitten which was still lying on the shed floor.

Even if the fight for food was a thing of the past, the survivors didn't normally just lie there when the parents went past. The youngsters usually backed off out of the way, having learnt a hard lesson from the death of the third kitten. But the kitten in the shed remained in a prone position. I watched it closely. After their aggressive spitting performance the adults returned to their meat stashed in the shed. As Fred walked past the kitten, it flinched back from the shoulders but didn't move its body. I stared. It would normally move away or crouch in submission. There was something wrong. I looked at its legs, which didn't move with the upper torso. I couldn't be certain but its legs didn't look as if they were lying right. They seemed to be too relaxed for the position of its upper body. The creature looked paralysed.

There was no choice; I had to go into the enclosure to check, and if it were sick or injured, somehow I had to get it out of the shed. If something was wrong, its fate would no doubt be the same as the third kit. I could not risk any delay; there was no time to get help or to prepare some protective clothing. It could be only a matter of time, possibly minutes, before the crippled youngster was targeted by one or both parents. Sick wild animals are frequently killed by the others in the group, a natural precaution to prevent the lame from holding up the group and placing all the family members at risk from either attacks by stronger predators, or even starvation due to delayed hunting.

The Kellas cats, either one or both, had killed their kits

before, and a crippled kitten had no hope of survival if it remained in the enclosure. But I had never dared to enter the shed itself: that was the adults' den and food store, even before the kits had arrived. I seldom now dared to enter the enclosure itself, so how was I going to get the kit out of the shed in an attempt to save it?

I dashed indoors and put on my heavy waxed jacket in the hope that it would deflect any attacks to the body, although it still left my legs, hands and face unprotected. I called Mandy, who luckily was home, and asked her to hold the outer door closed until I was out of the inner door. Whatever happened, she had to secure the second door to prevent the adult cats escaping. My one defence was a swiftly grabbed mop, the old fashioned kind with a soft head. Then I was ready. I opened the outer door and Mandy slammed it shut behind me as I entered the passageway. I unlatched the inner door and stepped inside, closing it behind me. There was no point in silence. Fred and Freda stood snarling, guarding their territory.

I thrust the mop towards them to distract them and advanced. Fred grabbed the mop head and hung on with teeth and claws, almost wrenching it from my hand. Freda made a couple of token lunges and then retreated to the den, disappearing inside and then reappearing at the entrance, snarling viciously. I ignored the intimidating display, hoping it would remain vocal and that she wouldn't take courage to attack my back as I continued to walk towards Fred who retreated still worrying the mop head. We reached the shed, Fred reversed in, snarling and lunging at the mop as I followed. I was now inside. I had never actually stepped inside the shed since the wildcats took up residence, I was no longer on any form of neutral territory, I was now a serious threat to the cats. Not only was their sleeping shelf within reach, I was also just inches from their food store. If they were going to attack with serious intent, it would be now. Fred looked at me horrified and paused in his attacks at the mophead, obviously considering the implications of my entering his private space. He stared at me, his golden eyes blank, almost hooded, and although he continued to spit and growl, he semi-crouched as if in partial submission. I had to act quickly, while Fred was undecided about his next move. Once I had made my intentions clear, that I intended to steal one of his kits, he could decide enough was enough and the attack would be in earnest. I was also painfully aware that Freda, her maternal instincts aroused, would be at my back. Speed was essential.

The kitten was crouched towards the rear wall, spitting, trying to wriggle away from me. I had been right. It could not walk. There was no time to lose. I bent down, keeping my eyes on Fred, and grabbed at the kitten, hauling it up by the scruff with my bare free hand. I had it!

I backed away, holding the mop towards Fred, and with the kitten wriggling and spitting in my free hand. I was out of the shed and within striking distance of Freda who was still snarling from the entrance to the the den. The next few seconds were a blur, I was across the enclosure and out of the first gate, flinging the mop to one side to secure the lock with my free hand. Mandy had the second door open and I was out, unclawed and with the spitting kitten held firmly aloft. The adult cats recovered from their shock and threw themselves at the closed door.

'Quick! Get the carrying box out of the caravan!' I yelled, acutely aware that the twisting, snarling kitten was in an insecure grip. It managed to spin round and sink its claws into my hand, but I hung on, amazed by its strength and ability to pivot its upper body in an attempt to bite me. Mandy ran across to the caravan and spent an interminable time turning the key the wrong way before finally wrenching the door open and hauling out the large carrying case. She wasn't a moment too soon, I could feel my grip weakening with the strain, the wriggling fur slipping through my aching fingers. Then the kitten was in the case and the drama was over.

I was shaking as I headed for a desperately needed coffee. While I had hold of the kitten I had been relieved to note that it wriggled with ease, kicking its back legs and lashing its tail. I was thankful that it was not paralysed and had not broken its back as I had feared. I considered a trapped nerve, a slipped disc or broken pelvis as possible causes for its sudden disability. What did cause me some unease, however, was lameness in the back legs of the other kitten. Could there be some genetic fault suddenly revealing itself? A bone weakness perhaps?

The kitten huddled in the back of the cage, half buried in the straw, gazing at me out of bewildered golden eyes. I gave it some meat strips and some milk and water and put the box on a table at the end of my bed. I thought if it could watch me sleeping it would feel less threatened by me. Animals frequently turn their backs on a threat situation and relax, showing that they are not feeling aggressive towards the other party and are not expecting to receive aggression.

It probably didn't help the kitten much but at least I felt I was trying to do something to reassure the terrified little creature. During the night I was constantly aware of its eyes shining in the darkness, its fixed stare never leaving me. I fell asleep knowing it was studying me intently.

The next morning I awoke to find its eyes still focused in my direction. It had made no attempt to eat or drink, and I was worried that it would become dehydrated from the lack of liquids. By mid-morning I had decided to try to feed it milk. While it remained crouched at the rear of the box I had to reach in towards it for the top of the box didn't lift off. At every approach it snarled and spat, tiny versions of the parents' pistol shot *Phaah*! I tried putting liquid in a long handled spoon and pouring it into the open mouth when it spat. It was only a small quanity of liquid that I managed to get down its throat with this rather haphazard method but I hoped the kitten would accquire the taste and try the milk for itself. It was the kitten that I had never seen taking meat, so I guessed it had not yet been weaned from its mother – and this gave me an added problem. With its temper, claws, teeth and age, bottle-feeding was out of the question. I thought it would be easier to spoon feed it in an open box so I decided to risk putting my hand into the cage to grab it by the scruff. By distracting the frightened kit with one hand, I reached in and grabbed it, hauling out the terrified spitting fury. I then made a misjudgement. Believing that the kitten couldn't walk, I placed it gently on the floor. It reared up and spat, then suddenly realised its freedom. Before I could stop it, it motored off at an amazing speed to scrabble half on its bottom, across the floor and under the nearest furniture. It took me the best part of half an hour to retrieve it from its hiding place. This time I placed it in a box from which it promptly climbed out. I gave up and put it back into the carrying cage.

By teatime it still hadn't attempted to drink on its own and had now learnt to clamp its jaws firmly shut at the approach of the spoon. Despite the fact it was Sunday, I decided the kitten couldn't hold out until the vet's surgery opened next morning so I rang the vet's out of hours number and got hold of John Deer. He agreed to see the kit immediately.

Examining the frightened kitten was not easy due to its capacity to almost rotate its head at a 180-degree angle in an attempt to sink its teeth and claws into the hand holding it by the scruff. As John wanted to see its movements we put it on the floor and he was treated to its speedy crablike scurry. However this time we were ready for it, although it almost got under the surgery sink unit.

Next, with me firmly hanging on to to its neck, it was stretched out on the table while John examined the injured leg. He also had our first look under the tail. The kit was female. She endured the indignity with very bad grace.

John shook his head. 'The leg is badly broken. I don't think it can be fixed. It will need pinning and even then . . .' he paused grimly . . .' I doubt if anything can be done. We might start to operate but find we have no choice but to put her to sleep.'

It was a bitter blow. I had hoped, when the spine appeared undamaged, that the kit would respond to treatment. The kit struggled to fight back at the humans restraining and prodding her. I looked at the frightened eyes gazing up at me and remembered her as a little bundle of russet chocolate fur tottering across the enclosure on her first day out of the den. One dead, one lame and now one facing the death sentence! The breeding programme was becoming a disaster.

'You will try?' I pleaded.

John shrugged. 'It will be an expensive operation and there will be no certainty of success?'

I flinched. Money was tight, but . . . I sighed.

'We must try. There are only these two kittens reared in captivity. We must try to save her.'

'I'll do what I can, but . . .' We both stared down at the struggling bundle of black fur. For the first time I noticed she had most of her black coat; only the head still revealed the telltale stripes, and even these were fading.

'When will you do it?'

'Now. There's no point in leaving the animal like that. I'll operate right away. You hold her while I get the anaesthetic.'

Five minutes later, the kitten's struggles ceased and she was put sleepily into the vet's cage. There was nothing more I could do.

'You go home now, Di,' instructed John kindly. 'I'll ring you whatever the verdict as soon as we find out if we can do anything.'

'How long?'

He smiled. 'An hour to an hour and a half and it will be finished, whatever the outcome. I'll ring you at home immediately it's over.'

I paused in the doorway. 'Do your best, John. A lot of people, including the scientists, are interested in her surviving. She's a very important little kitten.'

He nodded. 'I'll give it my best shot.'

I walked across the car park carrying the empty box and loaded it into the car. I felt helpless, almost certain the kitten would die. In tears I drove home to await the results of the life and death battle.

It was three hours before John phoned. The long wait had given me a glimmer of hope although I was afaid to tempt fate. It felt a lot longer than the three hours the clock assured me had passed.

I hesitated before lifting the reciever. 'John? How did it go?'

'Well, we've got it pinned and all we can do is keep her still and as quiet as possible and see how it goes. The operation went well. Are you coming up to collect her now?'

It was like hearing of a temporary reprieve for a prisoner under sentence of death. It was a reprieve but not a pardon. I drove to the vets with a lightened heart. The operation had gone well but she now had to be kept still for six weeks! And I had to persuade her to eat and drink.

But at least she was alive. The problems could be faced in the future. For the moment it was enough to take her home and let her sleep off the anaesthetic. If she recovered from the shock and trauma of the operation, and if she accepted food, then in ten days she was to be returned to the vet for the removal of her stitches.

That night I again slept with her box at the foot of my bed, but this time she showed no interest in her surroundings. It was I who watched her through the dark hours, listening for every faint rustle that would tell me she still lived.

Next morning I woke to the sound of birds, not from the trees outside my window but from the box in my bathroom. The bantam chicks were trilling for their breakfast. I looked at the kitten. She was stretched out motionless, her back against the wire of the door, her ears silhouetted black against the morning light. I stared, looking for some movement, some sign of breathing to tell me she was alive. The straw rustled slightly as she changed her position. I lay and studied her silent slumped shape and wondered how I was going to cope. How was I going to keep her restricted and dry and clean? That was, of course, if I could persuade her to eat and drink.

There was another problem. Whatever had occurred must

have involved an attack by one of the parents. The injuries of both kittens were to back legs and so I deduced they must have been caused by side swipes, blows heavy enough to break the kittens' fragile bones. Somehow I had to get the other kit out of the enclosure before it was attacked again. Next time it would almost certainly be killed, having already been weakened. But how? I had been lucky with the female only because the parents had been off guard, not expecting me to take away their young, and the kit herself had been unable to retreat away from me. Now the parents would be warned as to my possible intentions and the remaining kitten, although crippled, could still run at a fair speed.

It was not going to be easy, yet I was now certain that for the kitten to stay with its parents was to sentence it to death. At least I knew that it was eating meat and so could easily be weaned away from its mother.

Worrying did not improve the situation. I fed and watered the chicks and then saw to the feeding of the rest of the livestock before walking the dogs. A golden bantam was sitting in an unnatural position in the horse's field. I looked closely. She was one of the chicks I'd hand-reared when their mother had died after hatching them. I realised I hadn't seen her for a few days and had a nasty suspicion that all was too well. As I approached she held her ground until the last moment, rising abruptly and spilling half a dozen fluffy newly hatched chicks across the muddy ground. They had no chance with the cold wet freak weather conditions and the prowling cats. I gathered them up, finally catching mum, and shoved them all into the empty rabbit hutch.

Then, the chick crisis over, I turned my attention back to the crippled kit in the enclosure while the parents were in the shed. I decided to take the chance and go in for another quick grab. I was breaking my own rules for I had no one with me to get help if I were injured, but I felt it was worth the risk. I opened the inner door quietly and latched it behind me. So far, so good. The adult cats were dozing in the shed, unaware of my arrival. The kit crouched in front of me, hesitated as I made ready for the grab, and then shot away under the den at astonishing speed. I had no chance. I retreated quietly just as Fred became aware of me and came thundering out of the shed to see what was going on. I leaned on the outer door and stared at him spitting majestically in defence of his territory. I could do nothing to retrieve the kitten at that moment; it was a case of watching for a suitable opportunity and taking it when it arose. I could only hope it would come before the next bout of aggressive behaviour from the parents towards the defenceless kit.

All day the other kit remained huddled wearily in the back of her box, making no attempt to eat or drink. I hoped it was just the delayed effect of the anaesthetic that was keeping her so quiet, rather than physical weakness, but as she had taken nothing orally since I had grabbed her, and I had no idea how long she'd been without food before that, unless she at least took liquid it was only a matter of a couple of days before she would die. Perhaps less. Refusal of food was not dangerous for a few days yet but dehydration would kill swiftly. She *had* to drink.

I tried drops of milk in a long handled spoon but she just gazed at me wearily and turned her head away, keeping her jaws clenched firmly shut. Every hour or so I repeated the attempt, but with the same negative result. The only glimmer of hope was that she frequently changed her position slightly and so obviously had enough spirit to move around in an attempt to get comfortable.

She was still alive on Tuesday morning. I awoke to see her pricked ears silhouetted against the light. She was studying me. Her food and drink remained untouched. I tried again with the spoon, this time to be greeted with a furious *Phaah*! She was looking more alert and her temper had returned. She attacked the spoon, biting and clawing with her front paws. My hand felt at risk, being within range of the lashing paws but I held my ground although I frequently jerked back in fear at her onslaughts, spilling the drops of milk as I tried to pour it into the snarling red mouth. She might have been captive bred but she was all wildcat temper and definitely her mother's daughter.

In the afternoon she took her first tentative laps from the spoon, her rough red tongue rasping against the metal edge. Most of the milk spilled but she quickly learned the knack and soon drank eagerly, her bright tongue curling around her mouth after each session, cleaning the milk from her fur and nose.

The next day she accepted her first piece of raw meat, chewing it enthusiastically with low mumbling growls.

If the bone knitted around the pin and she stayed clear of infection, the operation was going to be successful.

15

Death in the Afternoon

Once she started eating, she appeared to be making up for lost time, devouring every scrap offered, but she never accepted the food without first giving a token display of ferocity, spitting with a loud abrupt *Phaah*! before delicately taking the juicy chunk from my fingers. She gave the same display before lapping from the offered spoon, but she would then allow my hand to rest against her curled body while she was drinking.

Nine days after the operation, she curled up comfortably against the bars, no longer retreating to the dark rear of the box. After giving her a piece of pork, I cautiously touched her flank, gently stroking her back and leg before closing the door. She gave no sign that she was even aware of me taking such a liberty. Of course she must have felt the pressure but was secure enough to ignore it.

For the first time I had actually stroked a Kellas! It was a moment of great personal satisfaction.

At the same time it was obvious that even when totally dependant on me for food and companionship, the Kellas cat did not accept captivity gracefully, nor was she willing to like humans. It seemed a point of honour in the species to continue their show of aggression. Any relationship formed with her would obviously be on her terms, not mine. I would have to wait until she revealed what those terms would be.

Meanwhile it was going to be far more difficult to catch the other crippled kit and remove it from the adults' enclosure. And having got it, where was I to put it? I couldn't put it in with its sister because she had to be kept as motionless as possible for six weeks. Isolated, she slept, for most of the time, moving in occasional shuffling circles to change position and make herself comfortable. She urinated on the paper at the back of the box and then shuffled back to curl up on the warm straw and lie staring around the room in an open-eye doze. Such limited movement might have been boring for her but the restrictions gave her leg the chance to heal. Add her litter mate and she would want to fight and play with it, and then she would constantly be using the repaired leg before it was ready to take her weight.

The ideal solution was to build a new enclosure for the two kits and put the second one in immediately it was taken from its parents, but that could not be done overnight, I needed physical help with the construction work. It was impossible to hold the heavy beams in position and nail them to secure them at the same time with the same pair of hands.

As long as I delayed building, the second kit could be killed at any time if subjected to another attack by which ever parent was responsible for the former injuries. I compromised and borrowed a cage. If I could get the other kitten out of the enclosure, it would have to remain in the second cage in my bedroom until the new pen was complete. It would mean my bedroom was going to be rather crowded and not perfumed with the odour of roses, but at least the surviving kittens would be safe.

First I had to catch my cat before I could cage it, and every day it remained with its parents was one more day of danger. I had no way of knowing the sex of the remaining kitten but I hoped it was a male that could be paired off with Kelly. If it was a second female, then it would be no use to the breeding programme for neither kitten could be mated to the father. Any female kittens from Fred would have to remain separated until a suitable mate was trapped alive.

Still, at least two female kittens could remain together in a shared enclosure. If I succeeded in rescuing the other kit, and it was a male, then it would be too young to be put with Kelly and it would soon need to be kept apart from its sister in case it mated with her. The answer was a divided new enclosure, one that could be partitioned internally or left as one.

Deciding on the solution to the problem was still a long way from actually achieving it. First I had to snatch the second kitten and the kitten remained in unsnatchable situations, either inside the den itself or else wriggling under it, both places making it impossible for a bare-handed grab.

Every morning I checked the enclosure for any evidence of violence having taken place during the night, dreading to find a second mangled black fluffy body. Usually the cats were resting up, the adults snoozing on the shed shelf or curled out of sight in the warm straw of the den. I would scan the heaped straw in the shed, searching for anything resembling black fur amongst the assorted abandoned rabbit skins and goose and chicken feathers that littered the floor.

Usually it was midday before I was relieved to spot a small round-eyed whiskered face peering out at me from the den entrance and I could relax, knowing that another night had passed without incident. If the weather was cold, windy or wet, however, the kitten could remain out of sight all day and the only way I could be certain it was still alive was to enter the enclosure at feeding time when Fred and Freda were occupied with tearing their meat to shreds in the shed, hoping to spot it in the darkness of the den before its parents spotted me. I was not always lucky. Sometimes Freda would take her supper into the den and sometimes Fred would remain stubbornly in the middle of the enclosure, his eyes watching my every movement, ignoring his meat, obviously suspicious of my intentions. On those occasions I had to remain ignorant of the kitten's fate until the next day, when I would be greeted by the tiny black face looking up at me once more.

Even after I had acquired a temporary cage for the third kitten it stubbornly remained deep within the den. I had made a sort of landing net using steel rods, wire and a piece of commercial fishing net in the hope of scooping the kitten up at any opportunity when I spotted it in the open but it continued to stay buried in the rear of the den, giving me no access to it although I could see it clearly. I wondered if its leg was worse, and whether it was now unable to leave the shelter, or whether it just felt more secure inside after I had failed to catch it on one of its infrequent trips to the outside world. I had to satisfy myself by dropping food into the den every evening when the adults were occupied with their own suppers, visually checking on the condition of the kitten as best I could and at least ensuring it wasn't starving to death.

The day arrived when the female kitten was due to have her stitches removed. So far, despite John's pessimisn, the leg seemed to be healing with no sign of infection, and the kitten, once she had recovered from the shock and trauma of the operation, was eating well although still giving me a full wildcat display of ferocity every time I approached her. I held out milk or water on a spoon for her under her nose. She would give a low growl, an explosive *Phaah*! and then lap the liquid greedily, each new spoonful being greeted with the same routine, always one spit and a constant growl. When she had taken enough, she would turn her head away. Her meat I cut into bite-size pieces, tossing them under her nose where she would take them easily, chewing lustily and gulping them down until she had her fill. She would push the final chunk aside.

I called her Kelty, although I don't think she really noticed her elevation from a number to a name.

By the selection of spits and aggressive growls, I gained the impression she did not appreciate her return journey to the vet. I don't think the vet was enthusiastic about the meeting either as she attempted to demolish the table and the vet with her teeth and remaining limbs. I held her firmly by the scruff and John snipped the stitches and gave the leg a gentle probe.

'Looks good so far,' he said cheerfully as he stretched the damaged limb. 'Any luck with the other one?'

I shook my head. 'Not so far. I'm still trying to get it out of the enclosure.'

Kelty refused any food that day, wriggling around as if disorientated. I was surprised to note that she seemed to roll onto her back when snarling at me. As there had been no anaesthetic for the removal of the stitches I found this rather odd behaviour and assumed that the loss of tension on the skin where the stitches had been gripping her had confused her.

That afternoon, Kelty having settled quietly to snooze off her uncomfortable morning, I decided to have another go at getting her hold of litter mate. I went out to feed the cats, giving Fred and Freda theirs before going to feed Kelly and entering the main enclosure to check the kitten.

Then I paused. Kelly's food from the night before lay untouched. My heart sank. Something was dreadfully wrong. Sometimes a small piece was left if I had given her too much the evening before, but she never left all her food. I bent down and peered through the wire into the den. Normally one could see only the tunnel of straw leading to her inner sleeping chamber, but this time I could see her back lying stretched out in the outer compartment. Either she was ill or dead. I couldn't tell in the darkness if she was breathing. I lifted the door out of its sliding rail and stepped inside the enclosure for the first time since releasing her into the cage. I braced myself in case she were to shoot out of the den in an attack, but nothing happened. I approached the den cautiously and peered inside.

I could see her quite clearly, lying full length on the straw, her back towards the den entrance. I still could not see if she was breathing and did not fancy the idea of putting an unprotected hand into an enclosed space with a living Kellas. I got a stick and gave her a gentle prod. Nothing happened. I took a chance and put my hand in to touch her flank, already certain about what I was going to find. Kelly, the beautiful, wild three-legged cat was dead.

As I lifted the body out, it was already stiffening. I laid her on the grass, seeing her clearly for the first time. For a dead cat she was in superb condition, her leg wound healed perfectly, her coat thick and glossy. Even her eyes were not yet milky with death, but brilliant, glassy bright. There was no evidence of vomit or mucus around the eyes or nostrils, nothing to suggest the cause of her death. She was the healthiest dead cat I had ever seen.

It was a bitter and totally unexpected blow.

I felt stunned as I carried her back into the house. She felt quite heavy, suggesting that her appetite had been good up to the twenty-four hours of her death, the absence of mucus around the nose and the clean brightness of the eyes ruling out the usual virus infections. Her tail area was spotlessly clean, with no sign of diarrhoea, and that ruled out a number of internal problems or a gradual deterioration of condition.

In all, the lack of symptoms seemed to suggest a sudden end, possibly a heart attack. I bagged her up and placed her body in the freezer for the museum to examine at a later date. Perhaps they could determine the cause of death.

It was a sad evening. I had hoped to mate a male kitten of Fred's with Kelly but now there was no new bloodline to cross-mate any issue of Fred and Freda. I did not know how old Freda was, only that she had been in captivity for eight years, so she could be nearing the end of the line. If she died, the younger Fred could have been paired with Kelly, and so kept the breeding programme going. With Kelly dead, if Freda did not see another winter through, then only the capture of a new live female could salvage the whole project. It was a depressing future.

While Kelty slept off the shock of her trip to the vet I lay awake watching her tiny slumped black form at the foot of my bed. If she survived, or if another Kellas was captured, whatever the sex, I could provide it with a mate. It was a setback but not total disaster.

Over the next two days I tried again and again to get the third kitten out of the enclosure. The loss of Kelly made it even more important to try to save the kitten, even if at present I had no unrelated mate for it. I was begining to worry a little about Kelty's progress. She seemed to have lost her former co-ordination of movement, constantly rolling on her side when approached with food and eating awkwardly with sideways movements of the head.

On Friday morning I decided to attempt a frontal grab at the third kitten, despite the obvious risks involved. I had the temporary pen ready and later it could go into Kelly's enclosure. I had the idea of wrapping a hand carefully in cloth and thrusting it into the den in the hope that the kit would imbed its claws into the material and get hooked while I lifted it out and grabbed it by the scruff with my free hand.

I was thwarted in my attempt by finding Fred in the den. A frontal grab on a kitten was one thing, tackling Fred in full health was another matter entirely. I retreated from the snarling vision of Fred, his massive head jammed in the entrance, and backed out of the enclosure. I would try again later. A couple of hours passed, and after giving Kelty some milk from the spoon I decided to try again for her litter mate. This time I was in luck, for both Fred and Freda were patrolling the enclosure. I entered and moved towards the den, my mop jabbing towards the cats to distract them. The routine had become familar. Freda crouched and snarled and spat viciously; Fred growled and lashed at the mop head almost as a token gesture.

I kept my eyes on the two in front of me until I was alongside the den, then I glanced down and saw the kitten lying curled and asleep at the back. Usually by this time in the proceedings it was alert and spitting, warned of my presence by its parents' hostility.

Then I saw a couple of flies buzz out of the corner and I had the sinking feeling that I was too late. Still watching the adults warily, I tapped the den side but there was no movement from the kitten half buried in the straw. I reached in and grabbed. There was no movement. I caught hold of the kitten and finally pulled it out of the den. It hung dull-eyed and limp in my hand and I was conscious of it still having body warmth. It had not been dead long.

Fred and Freda watched me almost impassively, as if they understood the kitten was beyond all protection or help. I carried it gently away, still keeping my mop at the ready, but neither cat gave more than a token display of aggression, I felt sure they understood that I was not robbing them of their young; nature had already done that. I secured the gates and sadly carried the tiny body back to the house to examine it before bagging it and placing it in the freezer. There was no sign of new injuries and no obvious sign of violence. At least it had not been set on recently by either of its parents, so my failure to retrieve it from the enclosure had not been a direct cause of death, as it would have been if the kitten had been attacked. There was a fresh stool tangled in its bushy tail, which also proved that my daily delivery of food into the den had been successful and starvation had not been a contributing factor to its death. Also it had not been suffering from any kind of enteritis. Like Kelly, it was clear-eyed and clean-nosed and did not seem to have suffered from a virus infection. I could only presume it had received some internal injury that had finally contributed to its death. I had guessed correctly that it was a male. I laid the tiny body next to Kelly in the freezer. The unrelated pair of cats were at last together, but not as part of the Kellas breeding plan.

Now Kelty was the only surviving kitten and she was far from healthy. As I fed her that night I worried about her condition. Since the stitches were removed, she seemed worse rather than better. She no longer crawled around or struck out at me with her forepaws, but lay passively when I fed her, even allowing my hand to brush lightly against her body without any reaction.

Still, at least she was eating, even if with difficulty and a lack of enthusiasm. But I did not like the way she constantly seemed to turn on to her back when I approached, rolling rather than crawling away from me. It had been three days since her stitches had been removed, and I could not understand why she should be having such difficulty moving around. I decided that if there was no improvement within the next twenty-four hours I would have to handle her to examine her, despite my reluctance to do so for both my own and her safety. I had only held her when I first caught her and during the visits to the vet. When cleaning her cage, I slid out the used paper and gently slipped in the fresh bedding in stages, with as little disturbance to the kitten as possible.

The next morning, Kelty seemed worse. She turned her head away when offered milk or water on a spoon. She had not eaten meat for twenty-four hours. I reached in, grabbed her by the scruff and gently hauled her out, turning her body in mid-air to examine her. I didn't have to look far to find problems. A steel pin like a giant needle gleamed where it protruded from her hip, sticking out about a quarter of an inch from the wound. I replaced her gently in the cage and phoned John Deer with the bad news.

'Bring her straight down and I'll have a look at her,' he told me consolingly. 'It might not be as bad as it looks.'

I looked at the tiny bundle of fluff gazing back at me with bewildered golden eyes. How much worse could it be, I wondered. Two kits already dead, the third crippled and getting worse instead of better. Kelly dead, Freda and Fred of unknown age but at least nine and six years old, if not a lot older.

Kelty growled as I picked up the cage. She knew what lay at the journey's end and she was not keen on the prospect.

John was waiting for me and within minutes of arrival I had grabbed her swiftly by the scruff and, while I held her firmly, John examined the repaired leg. He nodded.

'It's not as bad as it looks,' he said cheerfully. 'The pin's come unanchored but the leg is mending nicely. I'll have to operate again but I'm quite hopeful. We could have done without this little hiccup, but it is not a disaster.'

I breathed with relief. All was not lost. Within five minutes the kit was under sedation and on her way to another operation. This time it was over and she was ready for collection within an hour and a half. She offered me a violent spit and a growl as greeting while I loaded her into the car.

John smiled. 'I'll stand you this one as my donation to the research,' he said kindly.

I was relieved and thanked him. Besides the worry over the survival of the cats, my vet's bills were getting on the hefty side.

That night Kelty lapped her milk slowly from the spoon but refused to eat any meat. She still spat and growled and shuffled around in the strange rolling motion that had alerted me to the problem, but I assumed it was the effect of the anaesthetic which stays in the bloodstream a fair while. The poor little scrap had been through two major operations within a couple of weeks.

Two days later she was still crawling around with that weird crablike shuffle and roll, constantly ending up on her back. I was afraid to handle her and was sure something was wrong. I studied her weaving movement carefully. She seemed unable to grip with one front leg to drag herself round. I watched as the paw almost doubled under her. Either it was paralysed, or there was a trapped nerve, or she had injured the joint. I picked her up by the scruff and, holding her gently, touched the leg. It was loose and floppy, the paw drooping.

It was Sunday again, and I saw no point in disturbing John. Whatever was wrong, it had been wrong since she had had her stitches out, but we had not noticed it while concentrating on the rear leg. I would leave it until the following morning, before I rang John and told him the news. His immediate thought was nerve damage, and he asked me to bring her in. Once more we were on our way to the vet's.

When she had been examined before, it had been her back leg that had been the focus of attention. With me holding her firmly by the scruff of the neck, John was able to keep clear of her lashing front claws and bared teeth. To look at her front leg was a different proposition altogether as John's hand had to be within range of her bite. I suggested that we should fit a plastic collar of the type used to prevent animals biting themselves. It was not easy to thrust a wriggling, spitting

Kelty's head into the rigid funnel, but after a couple of false starts, the deed was done and the terrified kitten gazed at us from the depths of an uncomfortable plastic tube. John laid her on the table and lifted her injured paw gently, ignoring her struggles as she almost slipped from my grip. He shook his head.

'The leg's broken,' he said with a worried frown. 'I'll have to operate and pin it.'

Not just the back, but the front leg too! It was hard to take in as John gave her the shot of anaesthetic and I held her.

Within seconds, Kelty's frightened golden eyes grew sleepy and her body relaxed. John took her from me.

'I'll do it straight away,' he said. 'Ring me in a couple of hours.'

I reached out a hand and gently stroked the sleeping kitten. She had completely lost her baby coat and was jet black with a scattering of long white guard hairs, just like her parents. Her tail was a thick fluffy short brush, her whiskers long, framing her small delicate face. She was incredibly beautiful, my last little Kellas. I left the surgery, fighting back the tears as I drove home.

16

Looking to the Future

The telephone was ringing as I walked indoors. It was the vet's receptionist John had left a message saying that both front legs were broken. Both! It was too much. I asked if I could speak to John. Heartbreaking though it was, it seemed cruel to continue to try to save her, I felt it would be better to let her slip quietly away while she was asleep. But John was in the surgery, carrying out the operation, so I couldn't speak to him.

That evening I went back to collect her. John wasn't there but one of his partners carried out her box. Her tiny body lay stiff and still, covered with sheets of newspaper.

'She's gone,' I said sadly, expecting it but surprised they hadn't told me.

'No, she's fine, just covered to keep her warm. She hasn't come round yet,' he said. 'We had to give her extra anaesthetic so she's not with us yet, but the operation went okay, with no complications. Just keep her quiet and warm till she recovers.'

Kelty gave a little jerk as if to reassure me. I took the cage and drove home with her, wondering how I was going to cope with keeping her still enough for all three legs to heal. How had she managed to break the two front legs while she had been in isolation? It hadn't been violence on the part of the parents; it had to be something else. Were any of the kittens victims of the adult cats or was it more serious, perhaps genetic? Something that caused a form of brittle bones.

The night was long and terrible. Kelty writhed and convulsed, throwing her head back and arching her body, giving out high cries of distress like a wailing child. I sat up with her, talking softly, trying to soothe her, wetting my finger to moisten her lips and gums to help combat dehydration. She did not seem conscious of my presence. She appeared to be locked in a nightmare world of her own, screaming in terror from the horrors within her mind. As the dawn sun rose, she fell quiet and drifted into a more normal sleep. I hoped the worse was over.

Suddenly, she gave one last terrible scream, her whole body twisted and stiffened, and then it was all over. I lifted out the frail beautiful body and held it, my tears falling onto the soft glossy fur. My last little Kellas kitten was no more. I stroked her still warm body, searching for the last faint fluttering of life, but it was gone. I hugged her cooling body, cuddling her in death as I had never dared to do in life.

Later I wrapped up the cold little body and laid her beside Kelly and her brother in the freezer. The dream was at an end.

The death of the three-legged Kelly was the bitterest blow. It seemed almost certain that the kittens had died not due to any violent actions by the parents but because of a brittle bone condition passed on as a genetic defect by one of the adult cats. Had Kelly not died, then I could have attempted to mate Fred to her in the hope that the problem lay with Freda. If Kelly had produced kittens, and they also suffered from a bone defect, at least we could then have pointed the finger of suspicion at Fred and tried to obtain another mate for the females. If Kelly's kittens had remained healthy, then I could have continued the breeding programme, using her and not allowing Freda to breed again.

With Kelly dead and Freda old, the breeding programme was now uncertain to continue. The risk of brittle bones affecting a second litter of kittens made it unthinkable to carry on, putting yet more innocent animals through the misery that poor little Kelty had suffered during the final weeks of her short life. I could not forget the screams of that long and harrowing night when the little kitten had died, unable to cope with so much anaesthetic in her tiny body.

At first John had only given her a light amount, thinking he would have plenty of time as he had only one leg to deal with. When she was on the table, and he discovered the second break, he almost rang me to suggest he put her down. That had been my own response to the news. However, he decided to continue and set both legs, which obviously took longer than expected. Unfortunately Kelty had started to come round while he was still operating and she had to be given a further dose of anaesthetic. There was no way of avoiding it, but it was almost certainly that extra topping up that caused her failure to regain consciousness.

Even if she had recovered from that final operation, I couldn't see how we might have prevented her from suffering further breaks. John agreed with me; if she had a bone defect, then nothing could have saved her. We would only have prolonged her pain.

Could I really risk more kittens suffering in the same way?

We had already learnt a great deal about the black cats, which in turn gave us valuable information about wildcat behaviour. We knew the kittens were always silent, that when the mother greeted them, the kittens made no sound, even when suckling. Wildcat dens that seemed empty in the breeding season could be examined more closely now we knew that the kits would not betray their presence by sound. It was also notable that the mother appeared to visit them, rather than lie up with them, so an apparently unused den could indeed be very much in use.

Fred's behaviour towards the kits had also been interesting, for rather than being a danger, he had appeared tolerant and almost affectionate towards his offspring – a different image from that of the fierce kitten-killing tom that some people had suggested.

We could have learnt so much more if the kittens had grown up and been introduced into the wild, but I could not contemplate a repetition of the heartache and pain of the lost kits.

I discussed the problem with John Deer and Andrew Kitchener. They both considered it was worth another try before giving up, providing of course that Freda was young enough to be capable of producing another litter. They felt a second litter of kittens had a good chance of living normally, but despite their professional assurances, I could not help thinking of the lack of any surviving litters from the years when the two cats had been in the Highland Wildlife Park. If Fred had not killed them, or Freda eaten them because of the male's presence, why had the pair not produced and reared young during that period? Had a genetic defect caused the loss of all former litters? It was a worrying thought.

Later I received a phone call from Andrew, who thought he had discovered the cause of the kittens' death. It had nothing to do with genetics or hereditary desease, he said. It was dietary. Some people in Africa had encountered similar problems when rearing captive cheetahs. For the first five months the cubs had all appeared well, then suddenly, without warning, the healthy young became ill and developed rickets. The cause was so simple – calcium deficiency. The big cats had been fed on big juicy chunks of antelope, a plentiful supply of haunches, all tasty muscle material. With such an upmarket diet, the adult cats had thrived. But as the cubs grew older, they became deficient in calcium because their diet, though rich in protein, did not contain enough bone. They were given too much meat and were ignoring the less tasty but essential guts and bone. The cure was a reduction of best steak and an increase in the cheaper cuts. The problem had revealed itself only when the kittens reached the age of increased bone growth and began to lose the chubby cub shape, with longer limbs and heavier bones.

The Kellas kittens had thrived until four months old when they began developing into adult cats. I had overfed the adults good chunks of juicy beef and pork, thinking that there was less chance of well fed adult cats turning on their kittens. With so much steak, rabbit and chicken were discarded, rejected in favour of the more tasty morsels. By trying to do the right thing I had done the wrong; I had killed the kittens by over-feeding them with too good food.

It was a terrible feeling to realise that my own actions had caused the pain and the deaths of the Kellas kits. I had really killed them with kindness.

There was but one small grain of comfort. If Freda was young enough to produce another litter, then there seemed no reason why the young should not survive. The two cats had proved that they could do their part in rearing kittens successfully; it had been my mistake, not theirs. If the cats produced another litter, I would ensure that the diet was correctly balanced for the kittens' welfare.

The death of little Kelty would always haunt me, but if Fred and Freda survived another year, then next time . . .

It was winter. I had owned the Kellas cats for just over a year. During Christmas week the snow lay a foot deep and I had to go inside the cat enclosure every day to break the ice and refill the water dish. On Christmas day Fred sat in the frozen snow, his tail lashing from side to side just a foot from me as I filled the bowl, licking his lips with his bright pink tongue. Tiny icicles shone like Christmas decorations on his whiskers, his fur sparkled with frost. Freda peered out of the den with her usual snarl.

'Happy Christmas, Fred,' I said quietly.

Fred snarled half-heartedly. I looked into his huge golden eyes. There was no hatred there. He gazed back calmly, almost companionably. I knew I could never touch him but for the first time in a year I did not feel any fear. We had formed a bond of friendship; it was there between us, an almost visible link.

Appendix

Investigating the Identity of the Kellas Cats
by Andrew Kitchener

For ten years the Royal Museum of Scotland has directed research into the vexing problem of how to distinguish between Scottish wildcats, domestic cats and their hybrids. When I speak of hybrids, I include not only straight crosses between wildcats and domestic cats, but also all the complex crosses that occur in a mixed population. These are called introgressive hybrids. By using a number of different techniques – some new, others traditional – we have been able to make positive identification of eight black Kellas cats, seven provided as carcases by Di Francis and one in our own collection.

From the start, I decided to ignore their black fur and to examine carefully the rest of the morphological evidence. After all, melanism is commonly found in the cat family, even if it is very rare in species such as the puma and the European wildcat. The one disadvantage of this approach was that it precluded me from taking into account the pattern of stripes which can be seen in a normal-coloured cat to see if this conformed with wildcats or domestic cats or hybrids.

When investigating any cat, the first thing our taxidermists do is measure and weigh it. Then the animal is skinned and the pelt preserved for our research collections. Soft tissue samples are taken from the carcase and frozen for other research work, including molecular studies, toxicology and pathology. We also measure the length of a cat's intestines, for research in Europe has shown that there is a considerable difference in the length of gut in a wildcat compared to that of a domestic cat. But more of that later. Finally the skeleton is cleaned up so that measurements can be made to provide more vital clues to its identity.

The skull has four key characters that distinguish all wildcats from domestic cats. In other words there are differences in the shape and orientation of the bones of the nose, the brain case and the lower jaw. Hybrid cats, of course, have a mixture of these characters. So what did I discover about the eight Kellas cats?

It became evident from analysis of the Kellas skulls that one animal, a young adult male, had all four key skull characters of the wildcat. Another, a female, was very close to being a wildcat; she had just one character which was intermediate between a domestic cat and a wildcat. The other Kellas cats displayed a mixture of characters and so I had to conclude that these were hybrids, although most of the specimens were similar to wildcats. A multivariate statistical analysis of more than fifty skull measurements revealed two animals to have skulls similar in shape to those of wildcats which had been collected before 1940, when hybridization is thought to have been minimal. Even more exciting, these were the same skulls in which the character analysis had shown up as being wildcat, or pretty close to it. All the others came out as hybrids, but again several of these were fairly close to wildcat.

The length of the young male intestine turned out to be as short as a wildcat's gut can be, while the female had an intestine that was more than 60 per cent longer, a characteristic of the domestic cat. Nobody knows why domestic cats have much longer guts than wildcats, but it may have something to do with the less carnivorous diet of the domestic cat which needs a longer time for digestion to extract all the nutrients, and the simple way of achieving this is by having a longer gut.

Appendix

I also looked at the tails on the skins. A wildcat has a bushy tail with a blunt black tip and three to five complete black bands encircling it. I couldn't consider the pattern, but I could look at the overall shape. The young male had a typical wildcat tail shape, but the female's tail tapered, just like that of a domestic cat or a hybrid.

Thus, of the eight Kellas cats on which I was able to carry out all the tests mentioned above, one animal is clearly a melanistic wildcat. The others are hybrids, some of which are very close to the wildcat. One animal is much closer to the domestic cat.

If the range of variation in Kellas cats is compared with that in the whole Scottish wildcat and hybrid population, we see a very similar pattern. Only about one in five Scottish cats are true wildcats, the rest being hybrids ranging from close to wildcat to close to domestic cat. Most veer towards the wildcat end of the spectrum. It is clear from our studies that the proportion of true wildcats among normal-coloured and melanistic cats is roughly the same, although we could still do with a larger sample of Kellas cats to test this finding further. When previously I had made a study of three Kellas cats, I had come to the conclusion that these were all introgressive hybrids, but with only a 12.5 per cent chance of finding a pure wildcat, this is not so surprising. A much bigger sample has revealed the first melanistic wildcat ever recorded in Scotland.

There is one more morphological test to be carried out on the eight Kellas specimens – the volume of the brain case – but I do not think that this will alter the basic conclusions I have reached above.

A. K., Edinburgh
6th September 1993

Bibliography

Aliev, F., 'The Caucasian black cat', *Säugetierk Mitteilungen* 22, 1973

Campbell, J. G., *Superstitions of the Highlands and Islands of Scotland*, J. MacLehose & Sons, 1900

Cocks, Alfred Heneage, 'Wildcats Breeding in Confinement', *Zoologist*, Third Series, volume v, 1881

Francis, Di, *Cat Country*, David and Charles, 1983

—— *The Beast of Exmoor and Other Mystery Predators of Britain*, Jonathan Cape, 1993

Heuvelmans, Dr Bernard, *On the Track of Unknown Animals*, Paladin, 1970

Hills, Daphne, 'Black cat from Advie, Scotland' and 'Kellas cat', British Museum of Natural History reports, 1986

Jenkins, David, 'The Present Status of the Wildcat (Felis silvestris) in Scotland', *Scottish Naturalist*, vol 70, 1961

Kitchener, Andrew, *The Natural History of the Wild Cats*, Croom Helm, 1991

Kurten, Bjorn, *The Evolution of the European Wildcat*, Helsinki University, 1965

Morris, Desmond, *Catlore*, Jonathan Cape, 1987

Ricciuti, Edward R., *The Wild Cats*, Windward, 1979

Satunin, C., 'The black wild cat of Transcaucasia', Proceedings of the Zoological Society of London, vol 11, 1904

Tomkies, Mike, *Wildcat Haven*, Jonathan Cape, 1987